# Coordinating religious education across the primary school

# THE SUBJECT LEADER'S HANDBOOKS

Series Editor: Mike Harrison, Centre for Primary Education, School of Education, The University of Manchester, Oxford Road, Manchester, M13 9DP

Coordinating mathematics across the primary school
*Tony Brown*

Coordinating English at Key Stage 1
*Mick Waters and Tony Martin*

Coordinating English at Key Stage 2
*Mick Waters and Tony Martin*

Coordinating science across the primary school
*Lynn D. Newton and Douglas P. Newton*

Coordinating information and communications technology across the primary school
*Mike Harrison*

Coordinating art across the primary school
*Robert Clement, Judith Piotrowski and Ivy Roberts*

Coordinating design and technology across the primary school
*Alan Cross*

Coordinating geography across the primary school
*John Halocha*

Coordinating history across the primary school
*Julie Davies and Jason Redmond*

Coordinating music across the primary school
*Sarah Hennessy*

Coordinating religious education across the primary school
*Derek Bastide*

Coordinating physical education across the primary school
*Carole Raymond*

Management skills for SEN coordinators
*Sylvia Phillips, Jennifer Goodwin and Rosita Heron*

Building a whole school assessment policy
*Mike Wintle and Mike Harrison*

The primary coordinator and OFSTED re-inspection
*Phil Gadsby and Mike Harrison*

Coordinating the curriculum in the smaller primary school
*Mick Waters*

# Coordinating religious education across the primary school

Derek Bastide

FALMER PRESS
· Taylor & Francis Group

UK    Falmer Press, 1 Gunpowder Square, London, EC4A 3DE

USA   Falmer Press, Taylor & Francis Inc., 325 Chestnut Street, 8th Floor, Philadelphia, PA 19106

First published in 1999

**A catalogue record for this book is available from the British Library**

ISBN 0 7507 0613 9 paper

**Library of Congress Cataloging-in-Publication Data are available on request**

Jacket design by Carla Turchini

Typeset in 10/14pt Melior and printed by Graphicraft Limited, Hong Kong

*Every effort has been made to contact copyright holders for their permission to reprint material in this book. The publishers would be grateful to hear from any copyright holder who is not here acknowledged and will undertake to rectify any errors or omissions in future editions of this book.*

# Contents

Acknowledgments ix

Series editor's preface x

Introduction 1

## Part one
### The role of the religious education coordinator

**Chapter 1** The role of the RE coordinator 7

Coordinating religious education 7

**Chapter 2** RE coordinators speak 11

Who are the RE coordinators? 12

The satisfactions of the job 16

Some problems encountered 20

Personal needs 23

Future needs in school 25

## Part two
### What the RE coordinator needs to know

**Chapter 3** RE, the 1988 Education Reform Act and beyond 33

The context 33

RE in the Education Reform Act 35

The basic curriculum 36

The content of RE 37

The role of SACRE 40

Agreed Syllabuses 42

The model syllabuses 43

**Chapter 4** The aims of religious education 45

Teachers' views on religious education 46

How did this variety of views come about? 47

Spiritual and moral development 53
The aims of religious education 55

*Part three*
Writing a school policy for RE

**Chapter 5** Working with colleagues 59
Staff attitudes to RE 59
Developing the shared vision 63
Key features found in schools where RE is successful 63
Case study 1 65
Case study 2 68

**Chapter 6** Religion and the agreed syllabus 73
Religion as a seven-dimensional activity 73
The agreed syllabus 81
Issues for discussion 83
Conclusion 87

**Chapter 7** Writing a religious education policy 88

*Part four*
Developing religious education in the school

**Chapter 8** Planning the religious education curriculum 95
Long, medium and short term planning for RE — in outline 95
Long-term planning 96
Medium-term planning 97
Short-term planning 105

**Chapter 9** Monitoring and evaluating religious education 106
Possible strategies 107
Focuses for monitoring 108

**Chapter 10** Assessment, recording, reporting and
accountability 111
The purpose of assessment 111
Assessing in RE 112
Accountability 117

*Part five*
Useful resources

**Chapter 11** Books, artefacts, videos and ICT 121
Books for teachers 121
Books for the classroom 125
Stories 131
Appropriate themes in secular stories 135

CONTENTS

Artefacts                                                139
Posters/Photopacks                                       141
Videos                                                   142
RE and ICT                                               142

**Chapter 12** Visits and visitors                       144
Visiting religious buildings                             144
Visitors                                                 146

**Chapter 13** Some useful addresses                     151
Some main organisations                                  151
Major RE resource centres                                152
Publishers of RE material                                153
Posters, wallcharts and artefacts                        154

Index                                                    157

For Margaret, Bill and Susan

# Acknowledgments

Anyone who produces a book of this nature is in debt to various groups of people over a number of years. There are, of course, professional colleagues of various subjects and persuasions, both in the university and in the diocesan education team who have willingly shared ideas over a number of years. There are research assistants whose enthusiasm and energy has kept one up to date. There are generations of students, and not least there are teachers on in-service courses, who have asked demanding questions and often bubbled with ideas. There are pupils taught in school from whom one has learned so much. There is also that large number of authors who have spread their ideas through the written word. So wide is the field of influence that it becomes impossible to identify the sources of ideas and approaches: they have entered the soul.

Beyond this I am also very appreciative of the understanding and informed support of my wife, Judith, in this as in previous similar ventures.

# Series editor's preface

This book has been prepared for primary teachers, many of whom are not RE specialists by training, charged with the responsibility of acting as coordinators for the Religious Education curriculum within their schools. It forms part of a series of new publications that set out to advise such teachers on the complex issues of improving teaching and learning through managing each element of the primary school curriculum.

Why is there a need for such a series? Most authorities recognise, after all, that the quality of the primary children's work and learning depends upon the skills of their class teacher, not in the structure of management systems, policy documents or the titles and job description of staff. Many today recognise that school improvement equates directly to the improvement of teaching so surely all tasks, other than imparting subject knowledge, are merely a distraction for the committed primary teacher.

Nothing should take teachers away from their most important role, that is, serving the best interests of the class of children in their care and this book, along with the others in the series, does not wish to diminish that mission. However, the increasing complexity of the primary curriculum and society's expanding expectations, make it very difficult for the class teacher to keep up to date with every development. Within traditional subject areas there has been an explosion of knowledge and new fields introduced such as science, technology, design, problem solving and health education, not to mention ICT. These are now considered entitlements for primary children. Furthermore, we now expect all children to succeed at these studies, not just the fortunate few. All this has overwhelmed a class teacher system largely unchanged since the inception of primary schools.

Primary class teachers cannot possibly be an expert in every aspect of the curriculum they are required to teach. To whom can they turn for help? It is unrealistic to assume that curricular support will be available from the headteacher whose responsibilities have grown ever wider since the 1988 Educational Reform Act. Constraints, including additional staff costs, and the loss of benefits from the strength and security of the class teacher system, militate against wholesale adoption of specialist or semi-specialist teaching. Help therefore has to come from exploiting the talents of teachers themselves, in a process of mutual support. Hence primary schools have chosen many and varied systems of consultancy or subject coordination which best suit the needs of their children and the current expertise of the staff.

In fact, curriculum leadership functions in primary schools have increasingly been shared with class teachers through the policy of curriculum coordination for the past twenty years, especially to improve the consistency of work in language and mathematics. Since then each school has developed their own system and this series recognises that the one to which each reader belongs will be a compromise between the ideal and the possible. Campbell and Neill (1994) show that by 1991 nearly nine out of every ten primary class teachers had such responsibility and the average number of subjects each was between 1.5 and 2.2 (depending on the size of school).

These are the people for whom this series sets out to help to do part of their work. The books each deal with specific issues whilst at the same time providing an overview of general themes in the management of subject curriculum. The term subject leader is used in an inclusive sense and combines the two major roles that teachers play when they have responsibility for subjects and aspects of the primary curriculum.

The books each deal with:
- **coordination**: a role which emphasises harmonising, bringing together, making links, establishing routines and common practice; and
- **subject leadership**: a role which emphasises; providing information, offering expertise and direction, guiding the development of the subject, and raising standards.

The purpose of the series is to give a practical guidance and support to teachers, in particular what to do and how do it. They each offer help on the production, development and review of policies and schemes of work; the organization of resources, and developing strategies for improving the management of the subject curriculum.

Each book in the series contains material that subject managers will welcome and find useful in developing their subject expertise and in tackling problems of enthusing and motivating staff.

Each book has five parts.
1 The review and development of the different roles coordinators are ask to play.
2 Updating subject knowledge and subject pedagogical knowledge.
3 Developing and maintaining policies and schemes of work.
4 Monitoring work within the school to enhance the continuity of teaching and progression in pupil's learning.
5 Resources and contacts.

Although this book has been written primarily for teachers who are coordinators for Religious Education, Derek Bastide offers practical guidance and many ideas for anyone in the school who has a responsibility for the RE curriculum including teachers with an overall role in coordinating the whole or key stage curriculum and the deputy head and the headteacher.

In making the book easily readable Derek has drawn upon his considerable experience as a teacher educator, researcher, and RE specialist. His writing will help readers develop the managerial perspective necessary to lead others. The discussion on teachers' approach to religious education, sharing visions of RE and the case studies provided will contribute to the coordinators' task of developing RE across the school. This is most pertinent at a time when some threaten primary children with an ever narrowing curriculum in an attempt to raise test scores. RE coordinators will appreciate the skills and knowledge outlined in this book to keep RE lively and interesting in the primary curriculum.

Mike Harrison, Series Editor
September 1998

# Introduction

In most primary schools each subject in the curriculum has a designated coordinator with the responsibility of developing that subject in the school. In large schools some subjects may have two coordinators, while in small schools a single teacher may be coordinator for several subjects. The role of the teacher designated to coordinate religious education (RE) is no different from that of any coordinator: it is essentially to develop the subject in the school and through this to raise the level of the pupils' knowledge and understanding.

The post of RE coordinator is reasonably new in many primary schools. Although RE has been a compulsory part of the curriculum since the 1944 Education Act, it was often neglected in many schools and often so little coordinated that what was taught was left largely to individual class teachers. The changes in schooling ushered in by the 1988 Education Reform Act with its emphasis upon a child's 'entitlement curriculum' backed up by testing and inspection has led to a more strongly subject-based curriculum. The need to ensure that this curriculum can actually be taught has also led to increasingly detailed levels of planning and coordination. RE along with the other compulsory subjects within the curriculum has benefited from this development and there is clear evidence both from school inspection reports and surveys done by Her Majesty's Inspectors (HMI) that there have been marked improvements in RE in primary schools.

Although the term 'subject *coordinator*' is widely used, a more appropriate title would be 'subject *leader*'. Leadership includes coordination but goes beyond it and this is particularly important in RE as this is a subject in which many primary teachers lack confidence and look to be led rather than to be coordinated. It is therefore likely that RE coordinators will have to give considerable support to colleagues including guidance on subject knowledge.

This model of subject management in primary schools with each subject coordinated and led by a teacher responsible for it is probably more convincing in theory than in practice. The basic issue for many schools is that many existing members of staff have not normally been appointed on the basis of expertise in a particular subject. The school's senior management team has therefore had to allocate teachers to subjects in a way which fits best. Sometimes a teacher already has a subject strength; other times a teacher has had to build up a subject expertise.

Schools have probably had more difficulty in securing appropriate members of staff to be the RE coordinator than in some other subjects — although music and design and technology are probably in the same position. In a survey of primary RE coordinators undertaken in 1996, which will be discussed later, 10 per cent of RE coordinators held a specialist qualification while 26 per cent were headteachers who had taken on the role because there was no one else to give it to! Other people were chosen because they were religious believers, because they had an interest in religion, because they had multicultural experience, because it fitted with history and geography, and so on.

The role of the RE coordinator is particularly demanding because it is an area of the curriculum in which many teachers lack confidence in their own knowledge and understanding and at the same time it is a subject whose boundaries have expanded considerably as it has taken unto itself a greater range of religious traditions. Yet, if well understood and well taught RE is both an area of great interest and excitement for pupils and also an important contributor to the nourishment of their inner selves.

The aim of this book is to help RE coordinators, most of whom are not RE specialists by training, along the path of coordinatorship. While much of the work will involve generic subject management skills, no different from those of the English or art coordinator, there are particularly demanding issues in RE which relate to attitude and to knowledge. The end of the journey will be to raise and develop the pupils' knowledge, understanding and awareness of religion.

*Part one*

# The role of the religious education coordinator

**Chapter 1**
The role of the RE coordinator

**Chapter 2**
Religious education coordinators speak

# Chapter 1 — The role of the RE coordinator

The role of any subject coordinator, whatever the subject, is largely about influencing other people. The ideal coordinator is an enthusiastic model to colleagues; is knowledgeable about the curriculum area concerned; keeps up to date with developments at a local and national level; listens to and acknowledges colleagues' concerns; is prepared to start from the point colleagues are at and to work from these; is prepared to work collaboratively with colleagues and to offer support where it is needed; to be a *critical friend* (both supporting and challenging) and above all to have a vision for the subject in the school.

## Coordinating religious education

An RE coordinator needs to have:
- a clear understanding of the legal requirements which affect RE in schools and of developments in RE both locally and nationally;
- an understanding of both the aims and purposes of RE in the education of children as laid out in the local agreed syllabus and of how these might be implemented in the school curriculum;
- a developing knowledge and understanding of the nature of religion and of the principal religious traditions in Great Britain;

- an interest in and enthusiasm for religious education;
- the opportunity to provide in their own teaching a demonstration of good practice in the teaching of RE.

These should therefore enable the RE coordinator to:
- have a vision of how RE might be developed in the coordinator's particular school;
- lead whole school planning for the continuing development of RE in the school;
- spread enthusiasm among colleagues;
- provide support and advice to colleagues;
- plan and acquire resources necessary to support the teaching of RE in the school including books, artefacts, videos and posters;
- coordinate liaison with outside contacts, especially with speakers from religious traditions and with places of worship;
- monitor RE in the school;
- coordinate assessment and record-keeping in the school.

This list will provide the basis for the discussions in this book and a glance at the contents should show how this is being tackled.

Although the coordination of RE in a primary school should be no different from the coordination of any subject — and should be done in the same way as far as possible — it is only realistic to recognise that there are differences and these differences arise from a mixture of causes, some legal, some emotional and some hard to categorise.

The fact that RE, although it is in the *basic curriculum* and therefore required by law to be taught in school, is not part of the National Curriculum places it in a different category from the other subjects and busy teachers trying to fit all they have to do into the week are inclined to see it as more expendable. It is also possible for a teacher to opt out of the teaching of RE on the grounds of conscience — and that, again, places it in a different category from the National Curriculum subjects for which there is no such clause.

Over and above this, it is important to recognise that teachers' own personal experiences and attitudes are powerful factors. For a number of teachers religion is a difficult subject and, inevitably, unhappy experiences of religion especially in childhood affect their attitude to teaching RE. This largely affects the teaching of Christianity and incidentally an interesting feature of the current situation is that many teachers feel easier teaching about other religions than they do about teaching Christianity. Some others who are religiously committed are tempted to see RE as an opportunity for evangelisation.

Other teachers, too, misunderstand the aims of RE and imagine that they are expected to seek commitment in their pupils; which, of course, is difficult if they do not show the same commitment.

These are areas which the RE coordinator has to tackle if the subject is to be established securely in a school and they do often require patience and tact. Above all, there must be a willingness to discuss carefully and calmly what is expected of teachers so that they can see the need to separate their own beliefs and commitments from the task of helping children to begin to understand religions.

In addition to this there is widespread lack of confidence because of the broadening of the content of RE to include a range of religious traditions. This should be a less serious problem. It has arisen with all the National Curriculum subjects as they came on stream and, through INSET activities, through research and through practice, teachers have developed the necessary skills and knowledge. This should happen, too, with RE and will be a major responsibility of the RE coordinator but, provided there is good support and adequate information available, this should soon be overcome.

It is not the intention here to deter anyone from embarking upon the role of RE Coordinator but simply to recognise that there are issues which will arise in a number of schools and the coordinator will need to deal with them. There are many, many cases of teachers initially suspicious about the teaching of RE, a suspicion based upon a false or inadequate understanding of the aims of RE, who, once the light dawned, became effective and enthusiastic teachers of the subject to their pupils. Such a change of view is doubly gratifying to the RE coordinator.

## Chapter 2    RE coordinators speak

In 1995–96 a research project was undertaken at the
University of Brighton into the work of RE coordinators in
primary schools. The project had a number of focuses. One
was the separate interviewing of the RE coordinator and of a
classteacher teaching RE to his/her class in more than forty
primary schools. These were schools in which RE was judged
to be satisfactory or better and, because of financial constraints,
were all situated in five education authorities in the South-east
of England. Findings from this are reflected in this book as a
whole. Another focus of the project was to gain a broader
picture through the use of a questionnaire. In this focus, eight
English education authorities were selected representing,
north/south, rural/urban, multicultural/(virtually) monocultural
and prosperous/economically depressed. From each of these
education authorities fifty schools were selected at random.
Voluntary aided schools were excluded as they are not required
to follow an agreed syllabus. Of the 400 questionnaires,
addressed to the school's RE Coordinator and with a stamped
addressed envelope for reply, 219 (54.75 per cent) were
returned. This was undertaken in May/June 1996.

What follows here are some of the responses to aspects of the
questionnaire, namely:
■ Who are the RE coordinators?
     What academic qualifications do they have in RE?
     Why were they appointed to the post?

Do they have other roles in the school?
Are they happy in their role?
■ The satisfactions of the job
■ Problems encountered
■ Personal needs
■ Future need in school

These responses have vivified many of the issues which RE coordinators have found in the course of their work and have, therefore, contributed to the treatment of issues in this book.

## Who are the RE coordinators?

A developing feature of the past few years in primary schools has been the identification and appointment of teachers on a staff to coordinate and lead curriculum subjects and this has taken an even greater importance since the Education Reform Act of 1988. This process is not without its difficulties, two notable ones being the special position of small schools and the school with a very stable staff. In this sample, 13 per cent of the schools had less than 100 pupils and 40 per cent in all had less than 200 pupils. In one school, which has only 42 pupils and two teachers, the headteacher herself takes responsibility for RE along with six other subjects! In established school staffs, the allocation of subject leader roles is usually by negotiation and discussion as it is highly unlikely that a school would have a qualified specialist for each subject. On a stable staff it is only rarely that there is a teacher vacancy and then it is only possible to recruit a subject specialist if one applies. All these issues are relevant to the appointment of RE coordinators but they are also relevant to many of the other subjects on the curriculum. School management groups, in order to secure a subject spread, often have to look to the interests and enthusiasms of members of staff rather than the subjects which they specialised in when training. One large primary school has a gifted history coordinator who is an amateur archaeologist and secretary of the local historical society. Such experience and knowledge is seen by the school to be far more valuable than the science he specialised in during his training twenty-five years ago!

Among RE coordinators, 21 per cent of the sample had an appropriate qualification from student days. Two per cent had BA degrees in Religious Studies, theology or a kindred subject such as philosophy and a further 19 per cent had studied divinity/religious education/religious studies as their main subject in the BA(Ed), BEd or Certificate in Education. In addition to these RE specialists, a further 16 per cent had undertaken serious and sustained study of religions since their qualification as teachers. This included those who had undertaken certificates or diplomas in RE, ten or 20 day funded courses, an MA degree and various church-based courses such as training to be a local preacher or a Reader and the Bishop's Certificate of Christian Knowledge. In all 37 per cent of the sample had some form of formal qualification gained either during initial training or subsequently. To give some flavour to these figures:

> *The head invited me to be the RE coordinator so that I could use the knowledge and understanding gained in my religious studies degree to develop the teaching of faiths other than Christianity.* (County primary school, North-west)

> *I seemed the obvious choice on the staff due to my background in philosophy and ethics. Also I enjoy investigating religious ideas and encouraging children to do so.*
> (County primary school, West Midlands)

> *I am a Reader in the Church of England and to become that I had to undertake a substantial distance learning course. This fits me well as far as teaching Christianity is concerned though it did not do very much for other religions.*
> (County primary school, South-east)

Those noted above are in many senses obvious choices for appointment as RE coordinators; they have interest and also levels of knowledge and understanding beyond the normal. Where a school staff did not possess one of these — and this was in almost two-thirds of the schools — their school senior management groups had to look further.

One strategy was to look at other subject groupings and to see if RE would fit in any others comfortably. In some schools, humanities was seized upon and RE was placed with history and geography. While that may have served well as an administrative ploy, it did not necessarily work in practice:

*It was thought that RE would fit well with history and geography but it doesn't.* (County primary school, East Midlands)

In other cases, headteachers looked to colleagues with an interest in the subject or with previous appropriate experience.

*I had had multicultural experience in my previous job.* (County primary school, North-east)

*I was invited to be RE Coordinator because I had worked overseas in non-Christian areas.* (County primary school, South-east)

*Because of an obvious interest in RE.* (Country primary school, East Midlands)

*I would have been invited if I had not volunteered because I hold a 'global' view of RE.* (County primary school, East Anglia)

If no one in a school staff fitted into these categories, headteachers tended then to look towards colleagues who had religious commitment — and religious commitment was often defined in terms of going to church. This would be done in a crass way:

*The headteacher at the time said that he thought that I was the most 'religious' person on the staff (I don't necessarily think this is a good criterion!!).* (County infant school, East Anglia)

*I was seen as the obvious candidate as my husband's father is a retired vicar!* (County infant school, South-east)

In milder forms this was a very common motivation.

*I am the oldest member of staff and a regular churchgoer.* (County primary school, East Anglia)

*Because I am a Christian and go to church.* (County primary school, West Midlands)

❛ *I was a C of E churchgoer and was tactful!*

(County primary school, West Midlands)

In many ways, if a school does not have an RE specialist on the staff, this is probably the most realistic strategy. It is reasonable to suppose that a teacher committed to, say, Christianity or Islam, is likely to have a deeper understanding of the nature of religion than many, but RE coordinators in this category were also deeply aware of what they also lacked. As one recently appointed RE coordinator put it:

❛ *I am a practising Christian so I feel that I have a good aware-ness of a religion from inside and I am a Sunday School teacher so I have a reasonable level of knowledge of aspects of Christianity but I do lack knowledge of other religious tradi-tions and also I have no up-to-date understanding of what RE is trying to do. I'm going to have to do some hard work!*

(County primary school, South-east)

Headteachers still tended to make the simplistic judgment that being religious was enough to be an RE coordinator though a teacher who is a racing cyclist may not make the best PE coordinator nor a gourmet the best food technology coordinator!

❛ *The arbitrary share of subjects in a small rural school.*

(County primary school, East Midlands)

❛ *Needs must.* (County primary school, South-east)

❛ *A process of elimination — I am the headteacher.*

(County primary school, East Anglia)

This situation evoked a variety of responses ranging from:

❛ *I've no personal commitment to teaching RE — it's waste of my time.* (County infant school, East Midlands)

to

❛ *It's the first time I've worked in a school and been able to teach RE.* (County primary school, East Anglia)

> When all else fails headteachers themselves have had to take over the role of RE coordinator.

15

Of the whole sample, almost a quarter (50) of the RE coordinators were headteachers. Of these 35 were content with the role and the remaining 15 to some degree resentful. Of the whole sample only 23 (10 per cent) expresses dissatisfaction with their role as RE Coordinator in their school. In fact, many who had started off rather hesitantly and uncertainly had found satisfaction in the role, especially those who had had sufficient time to develop greater personal knowledge and understanding and had had some success in seeing RE becoming established in their schools.

It is interesting to note that 63 per cent of respondents regarded themselves as 'religious' with a further 3 per cent who preferred the term 'spiritual'. Thirty-one per cent claimed not to be religious. Fifty-three per cent claimed membership of a religious body (e.g. a church) while 44 per cent had no such affiliation. While such considerations are strictly irrelevant when considering provision for RE in the county school, it is useful to note that the percentage of those who call themselves religious and who claim a religious affiliation is significantly higher than among teachers as a whole.

## The satisfactions of the job

The overwhelming number of respondents recorded examples of satisfaction in the job with the exception of 13 (7 per cent) who said there were none or that it was too early yet to say. The remainder identified a considerable number of satisfactions in the job which can be divided into four areas: personal satisfaction, satisfaction with the responses of colleagues, satisfaction with the development of the subject in school and satisfaction with the response of children.

In terms of personal satisfaction, RE coordinators noted a quickening interest in the subject as they delved into it more deeply.

> *I have had to do a lot of research to help me to do this role satis-factorily and it has been extremely enjoyable.*

(County infant school, North-west)

Many has not been aware at the outset how interesting they would find the subject and with this enhanced interest came greater levels of enthusiasm for RE. Many noted the fascination of making first visits to places of worship of a variety of religions and had the opportunity to meet members of different faith communities.

> *I had never really realised before — though I must have known — how many mosques and temples there are in Britain.*
>
> (County junior school, North-west)

> *I shall never forget my first visit to a Hindu temple. The images were so beautiful and the devotion of the worshippers as they brought their offerings, was moving.*
>
> (County primary school, South-east)

With regard to the satisfactions derived from the work of colleagues, these certainly increased as coordinators began to see RE taking root more strongly in the school. There was great pleasure in 'the rolling back of the barriers of prejudice and apathy' (County primary school, South-east).

In some schools the prejudice was against Christianity, in others again the other world faiths and the apathy was largely born of ignorance of the nature of the subject. One coordinator noted:

> *It is good to see others spreading outwards from a 'narrow' Christian viewpoint.* (County primary school, East Anglia)

Helping colleagues to overcome their worries and uncertainties and to begin to plan appropriate RE encouraged RE coordinators to carry on with their work.

> *It is a great pleasure to support other staff in what they regard as a difficult subject — and to see their appreciation of my efforts!* (County primary school, South-west)

> *The real joy in supporting colleagues is to see their confidence develop.* (County infants school, East Anglia)

For many coordinators it was the satisfaction of seeing colleagues carrying out the scheme of work:

> *It was seeing colleagues carrying out our RE scheme of work and finding it not so bad after all that gave me the greatest satisfaction — and this was at a much greater level than I received on the other subjects I coordinate in the school.*
>
> (County primary school, South-west)

Some had moved beyond this stage and were working on the development of teachers' skills still further:

> *Now that colleagues are teaching RE from the scheme of work, I am now stimulating them to tackle RE in more interesting ways.* (County primary school, East Midlands)

Equal to the satisfaction felt with the progress in RE which colleagues were making in their teaching was the gratification which many coordinators felt about the enhanced position of RE in both the school curriculum and school life. Satisfaction was felt at 'getting things going', 'enabling RE to be taught', 'raising the profile of RE' and 'seeing it all running well'. Other coordinators were pleased with the way that they had developed approaches for teaching world religions successfully in their schools and of 'making RE interesting and relevant to the world we live in.'

A highly specific satisfaction was the acquiring of resources, especially books and artefacts. Because RE had only begun to be developed as a subject in very recent years in many schools there had never been any accumulation of resources (with the possible exception of a set of 'dog-eared' Bibles). Resources were widely needed in order to support the teaching:

> *Getting £300 to buy resources!* (County primary school, South-west)

> *Developing resources and seeing them used.*
>
> (County infant school, West Midlands)

Perhaps the deepest professional satisfaction was felt by those coordinators who had seen RE in their schools moving from the position of a fringe activity depending upon the whim of a headteacher or individual class teacher to one where it was now firmly embedded in the curriculum of the school.

> *It is a great satisfaction to see that RE now has a specific place in the school.* (County primary school, East Anglia)

> *It is a great pleasure to see RE become a regular lesson in the curriculum.* (County primary school, West Midlands)

> *Seeing that RE is now becoming an integral part of the curriculum with the same weight as other humanities.*
> (County primary school, South-east)

One RE coordinator went even further:

> *Seeing RE make a difference to the ethos of the school.*
> (County infant school, North-west)

The fourth broad area of satisfaction focused upon the pupils themselves. There was very broad agreement here that when it is well planned and well taught, children actively enjoy RE. There was very little evidence here of a confessional approach, whether open or covert, with ardent teachers wishing to induct their pupils into Christian faith. A number felt that they were in a privileged position because they are able, with many pupils, to provide a unique experience:

> *I am teaching about Christianity and other religions to children who will hear of them from nowhere.*
> (County primary school, South-east)

In this context RE is seen as a broadening experience, attempting to open pupils' eyes to a wider perspective than might emerge in a more narrowly focused utilitarian curriculum.

> *My great pleasure in RE is helping children to develop their spirituality.* (County primary school, West Midlands)

Others found great satisfaction in 'getting children to think!' This point was made most fluently by the deputy head of an East Midlands county primary school, who was also its RE Coordinator:

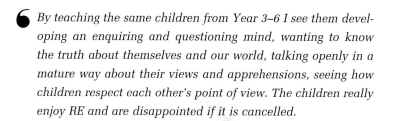

*By teaching the same children from Year 3–6 I see them developing an enquiring and questioning mind, wanting to know the truth about themselves and our world, talking openly in a mature way about their views and apprehensions, seeing how children respect each other's point of view. The children really enjoy RE and are disappointed if it is cancelled.*

## Some problems encountered

Whilst 20 per cent of the respondents admitted to no particular difficulties encountered, others were able to identify areas which had caused them problems and these tended to centre around colleagues, time, resources and, in some cases, themselves.

'It's getting colleagues on board. The children enjoy it!' (County primary school, Midlands) summed up many responses. Difficulties with colleagues was the most consistent concern, though it was clear that this tended to diminish with time as RE became more established in a school. Difficulties arose from a misunderstanding of the aims of RE in school, from a lack of knowledge, from a lack of confidence in dealing with religions and religious issues, from ambivalent feelings towards religion.

Many respondents noted misunderstandings about the nature of RE

*Responses ranged initially from 'I can't teach RE, I'm not a believer' to 'I don't think RE should be taught — it's up to the parents'.* (County primary school, North-east)

Many teachers thought that they were expected to teach RE along confessional lines.

This was further reinforced by a confusion between RE and collective worship. This appeared both as 'They do enough in assembly, why do I have to do anything more in the classroom' and also as a reinforcement of the RE/collective worship confusion:

*Saying prayers implies that God exists, so I don't feel comfortable teaching RE.*

Although this might appear a *non sequiter*, it was a broadly held view. Subject leaders felt that they had to challenge this viewpoint before they could move to the planning of RE in the school.

As it became clear in many schools that the county agreed syllabus required that pupils be introduced to a range of religious faiths, many members of staff became increasingly aware of the limitations of their own knowledge and understanding of religions. Teachers in the school where 'my staff think RE is Bible stories' (headteacher, county infant school, North-west) were suddenly finding that Judaism or Islam was on the syllabus. This lack of confidence on the part of teachers inevitably made teaching RE, at least initially, less enjoyable and this was easily communicated to the pupils. The anxiety though was often related, certainly in multicultural schools, to a fear of causing offence:

 *Colleagues worry over adequately covering religions of which they have scant knowledge. Anxiety over 'treading' on toes of religious faiths — offending without meaning to or even realising.*
(County primary school, London)

and perhaps with a slight bitterness

 *Getting flak from members of religious groups studied who see it as a point of principle to point out mistakes!*
(County primary school, Midlands)

Whereas many teachers felt uneasy about teaching RE because they felt their knowledge and understanding to be inadequate to the task, there were among some teachers deeper feeling which affected both their attitude and their practice:

 *It is difficult to make some colleagues feel comfortable about teaching parts of it, particularly those connected with Christianity (because of childhood experiences).*
(County primary school, North-west)

but also

❝ *I have two colleagues who describe themselves as 'born again Christians' and they are very resistant to dealing with any of the other religions in the classroom.*

(County junior school, South-west)

RE Subject Leaders found these two attitudes the most difficult to deal with.

The resistance to the teaching of RE on the part of some colleagues often found expression in the complaint that they are busy enough delivering the subjects of the National Curriculum without having to deal with a non National Curriculum subject — and a subject that demanded such a wide range of knowledge as well!

In addition to this reluctance on the part of some teachers, a number of respondents noted a suspicion in some governing bodies and among some parents to the teaching of other religions than Christianity.

❝ *In my school, there is a strong bias among the parents to teaching about Islam or Hinduism.*

(County primary school, Midlands)

❝ *In our school, we have noticed an increasing tendency for Christian parents to withdraw their children from RE because they do not wish them to have a knowledge of Hinduism until the secondary school.* (County primary school, North-east)

It was against this background that RE coordinators had to operate. They had to address the issues already identified: to deal with misunderstanding; to enthuse teachers unconfident with the subject; to prepare a school policy for RE and to develop a scheme of work. This was the challenge, but a number of RE coordinators did not feel that they themselves had an adequate armoury to deal with all these issues. Some of them felt that what they lacked was partly subject knowledge, partly time and partly a lack of resources to support the new developments in RE. One RE coordinator stated it succinctly:

❝ *Not enough expertise in my own knowledge of RE or time in school to plan the scheme of work — no budget to order resources.* (County primary school, South-west)

The evidence from the research suggests that these are not insuperable problems. The nature and content of RE has certainly developed and broadened and many RE coordinators have been able to develop and broaden their own knowledge and understanding in a variety of ways. Time allocation to undertake the work is partly a school management issue as is also the allocation of money to acquire resources which support the teaching. Responses indicate that in a large number of primary schools, RE is now settling into place alongside the foundation subjects of the National Curriculum. In fact, a number of RE coordinators, having already established a policy and a scheme of work, and had staff cheerfully teaching *about* religions, were now developing work which focused upon learning *from* religions. Others were devising approaches to both monitoring and assessing RE in their school. Much does depend upon the drive and enthusiasm of the RE coordinator, but much also depends upon the management of the school in its provision of time and money. Teachers, too, cannot resolve their misunderstandings and learn the necessary subject skills to teach RE confidently overnight. Patience is necessary.

## Personal needs

All the personal needs for development identified were concerned with a demand for greater training but there were two exceptions. One of these was to do with the need for more time — and this will be discussed later — the other arose from one desperate RE Coordinator who was attempting, with great difficulty, to activate a very stubborn and negative staff — fortunately this was the only such cry:

 *Prozac — and I'm not joking.*

(RE coordinator, County primary school, East Midlands)

A large number of RE coordinators felt that their knowledge of religions was inadequate, whereas classteachers could, without too much difficulty, read up the RE material they had to teach to their own class. Coordinators felt that they really ought to have a knowledge of religions that is both broad and deep.

> *I would really love to go and study this area further, such is my enthusiasm now for the subject.*
>
> (County primary school, North-west)

> *My greatest need is for courses — particularly on other religions.* (County primary school, North-east)

> *Learning about each of the religions so that I don't have to look it up all the time!* (County primary school, West Midlands)

While personal knowledge of subject content was highest on the list, demands for more specific training in being an effective coordinator were also very prominent. Again, the specific areas which needed developing depended to some extent on how far individual coordinators had been able to develop RE in their schools. Concerns ranged from how to go about organising and conducting RE development work with colleagues, including an RE inservice day; to formulating an RE policy document; to developing a scheme of work; to gaining an awareness of available resources; to monitoring and to assessing.

> *Training on ideas of how to approach certain aspects of religions.* (County infants school, South-east)

> *Contact with other schools' coordinators who are prepared to share schemes.* (County primary school, South-west)

> *Advice on useful/appropriate classroom resources.*
>
> (County primary school, South-east)

> Time *to prepare a quality curriculum plan.*
>
> (County primary school, South-west)

This final quotation with its emphasis upon *time* points to an issue which becomes even more prominent when RE coordinators reflect upon their future needs in schools. Many know what they would like to do — but lack of time prevents this again and again.

# Future needs in school

There can be no doubt that RE coordinators pinpointed the basic need as:

❝ *Raising the profile of RE in the school.*

(County primary school, North-east)

Earlier in this chapter this concern featured strongly in the accounts given of problems encountered. There was a wide concern that colleagues should see RE in the context of the whole curriculum and to begin to see connections with other subject areas:

❝ *To raise awareness of RE in school and for colleagues to see its importance in all areas.* (County junior school, South-west)

Allied with this was a clear desire to enable colleagues to broaden their understanding of what RE itself is now attempting to achieve.

❝ *To help staff to share my new enthusiasm (gained from a 10 day course) for this subject and to help them to understand that RE is more than a Bible story and a picture!*

(County primary school, North-west)

Staff training was identified as a key need if attitudes were to change and RE was to receive the boost it needed. Here again, shortage of time — or other priorities — was a constant theme.

❝ *If RE is going to develop in the way the Agreed Syllabus requires, then we need time to train the staff.*

(County primary school, South-west)

A newly qualified teacher in a county primary school in the North-west with a degree in religious studies put it plaintively:

❝ *I would really like an INSET day to boost RE and from someone who has more 'clout' than I have — but time and money!*

Further inservice work was also necessary if the development of RE was to be carried through to some form of fruition:

> *We have made a good start but what we need now is more INSET to keep the impetus going.*
>
> (County primary school, East Anglia)

This impetus was needed in a number of schools:

> *To complete the scheme of work and get it all up and running.*
>
> (County primary school, South-west)

In other schools, support in terms of inservice opportunities was necessary to secure:

> *the cooperation of colleagues in preparing for a review of the RE policy.* (County primary school, West Midlands)

Given the broadening of the RE curriculum it is very predictable that extension of staff knowledge and understanding of religions would be seen as an important need of most schools, partly because of its effect on teacher confidence and partly because it is essential if RE, as now required by agreed syllabuses, is to be implemented.

> *What we need more than anything else is a more detailed knowledge of major religions.* (County primary school, West Midlands)

In some schools, while this was identified as a major need it was not being addressed:

> *Our staff really does need knowledge but our budget does not stretch to this. We have other priorities.*
>
> (County primary school, East Anglia)

In such a situation where different subjects were competing for limited resources and RE was not a high priority, coordinators looked more to resources in the form of books and artefacts as a means of supporting RE. While it would be unrealistic to expect colleagues to gain a detailed knowledge of all the major religions, RE coordinators could be in a position to support them in the actual RE they were expected to teach to their classes:

❝ *My school's most realistic need is for me to build up resources for RE and to sort them into packs with themes and topics.*

(County primary school, North-west)

❝ *To build up resources and banks of information pertinent to each year group.* (County primary school, South-east)

These resources, given limited funds in school, would need to be focused:

❝ *A clear set of resources in line with the curriculum.*

(County primary school, West Midlands)

In this way, classteachers will be able to develop their knowledge and understanding of those parts they will actually teach and will have on hand both books and artefacts to support their teaching. One RE coordinator in East Anglia noted that he had also developed a list of suitable and appropriate visitors to make additional contributions.

Artefacts have for some time now been an important ingredient of RE teaching and are particularly useful for non specialist teachers as they can act as hooks upon which the teaching can be hung. Building up a supply of artefacts however is expensive:

❝ *I desperately need artefacts. I have no capitation allowance (honestly!!).* (County primary school, North-west)

Given limited financial support, some RE Coordinators had sought other and cheaper ways of securing artefacts than through the usual agencies:

❝ *I went one Saturday to some of the shops which serve the ethnic minority communities and gathered together a very useful collection at a price way below that of the catalogues.*

(County primary school, East Midlands)

❝ *I had a marvellous morning in the Portobello Road and picked up lots of second-hand artefacts all going for a song.*

(County junior school, South-east)

Because of the cost of purchasing resources, some schools, mainly in rural areas, considered that there was a strong case for building up collections of resources in clusters:

> *As a head in a cooperative cluster of schools I would like to take the lead and initiate inter-school loan of resources, particularly in the main religions.* (County primary school, South-west)

Throughout the responses there was a concern from many coordinators that they were being held back in developing RE in their schools by shortage both of time and of money 'I need *time* to coordinate properly' summed up the plight of a substantial number of RE coordinators:

> *I have no time allowance at all. This means that any support I can give to colleagues has to be done after school, in the lunch hour or at playtime. Many's the time I've explained the use of an artefact to a colleague on the hop in the corridor.*
>
> (County junior school, West Midlands)

The lack of time, especially where RE is accorded a low priority, can affect some schools much more seriously:

> *Because very little time was allowed in my school for the development of RE, I was left to write the policy and then to devise the scheme of work. This involved me in a considerable amount of work. It wasn't that that I objected to. The real difficulty was that my colleagues played no part in the development of RE. Certainly, they 'rubber-stamped' the policy with minimal discussion at a staff meeting but they don't 'own' it. I'm not sure that many know what's in it!*
>
> (County primary school, East Midlands)

Schools in this situation were few in number. More common was the cry:

> *I am not allowed any non teaching time so I can't get into other classrooms to monitor what is going on.*
>
> (County primary school, South-west)

Although surveys of this kind have their limitations, an interesting and positive picture begins to emerge.

❛ *If I am going to develop guidelines for teacher assessment of pupils in RE — and this is something I really ought to do — then I will need time to discuss and plan with colleagues.*

(County primary school, South-east)

Time and money came out very strongly as key needs for the schools.

A large majority of the RE coordinators who responded are enjoying their role, are extending their skills and knowledge and are finding that in most cases their work is beginning to bear fruit in both the developing understanding of RE among their colleagues and in the increased amount of RE actually being taught in their schools. Inevitably there are some difficulties especially over the attitudes of individual colleagues and on time and resources but the responses show that much can be done even in the most unpromising situations. Experiences drawn from here will be reflected in the rest of this book.

# *Part two*  What the RE coordinator needs to know

**Chapter 3**
RE, the 1988 Education Reform Act and beyond

**Chapter 4**
The aims of religious education

# RE, the 1988 Education Reform Act and beyond

## The context

Historically there has been a close link between church and school in England. Before 1870, the date when Parliament approved the plan to provide compulsory education for all, most schools had been founded by religious bodies and provided the appropriate religious teaching. With the arrival of the 'Board schools' provided by the School Boards set up in each locality to fill the gaps in the existing voluntary provision, the question naturally arose as to the form of religious teaching which should be given in these schools which were paid for out of taxes and had no allegiance to any of the churches or denominations. An agreement was reached (called the Cowper-Temple clause) by which the religious teaching given should not be 'by means of any catechism or formulary which is distinctive of any particular religious denomination'. If such teaching was not possible it was therefore necessary to find areas of agreement and one of the key features of Christianity upon which all the main churches and denominations agreed and which was not distinctive to any of them was the Bible. From this arose the great tradition of scripture teaching which dominated RE in English schools for almost a century. Although religious teaching was never in this period mandatory, it was virtually, if not completely, universal.

The 1994 Education Act was a great step forward in RE — or, to be more precise, RI as it was called then. This act made the following references to religion

■ that religious *instruction* should be given in every county school;

■ that each school day should begin with an act of worship;

■ that in each school there should be a right of withdrawal for both teachers and for parents on behalf of their children;

■ that each local authority should formulate its agreed syllabus for religious instruction (or adopt that of another LEA).

Although the 1944 Education Act did not lay down what it considered should be the aims of religious teaching or give guidelines for its content, there seemed to be an implicit assumption that the teaching should be, to use a technical term, *confessional* (that is, to attempt to lead pupils into a commitment to the Christian faith). Evidence for this is provided by the term *instruction* and by the right of withdrawal on the grounds of conscience for both teachers and parents on behalf of their children. For the 44 years from 1944 to 1988, the requirements of the 1944 Education Act were in place. During that time however much happened which began to change the ways in which RE was both understood and taught. Of these, two movements seems to be the most significant.

Firstly in the 1960s there was a considerable research focus on the way children's understanding of religious concepts developed. Of these researchers Ronald Goldman was certainly the most influential. Goldman argued that much religious material taught in school was drawn from the Bible and that many of the concepts therein were often too difficult and complex for children to make proper sense of. The net result, he claimed, was the misunderstanding by significant numbers of children of many religious concepts and these misunderstandings were often reinforced by further unimaginative teaching. Goldman argued strongly for a shift away from Bible-centred RE to child-centred RE and he recommended the exploration of topics such as bread, water, families, light, sheep and shepherds which were much closer to children's own experience and would therefore be more appropriate vehicles for pupils, especially younger ones, to explore religious ideas and concepts implicit in these topics. Goldman's ideas have almost certainly brought both benefits and disadvantages to RE teaching but they had considerable impact in that period and made very many teachers — and agreed syllabus compilers — think very carefully about the appropriateness of much of the content of traditional religious teaching.

The second was a change in the religious composition of the country. This was in part a loosening of the connections of many people with the main churches. Some of the traditional indicators of religious practice — churchgoing and baptisms, for example — were declining and it was becoming much more acceptable to admit publicly to agnosticism. At the same time other religious traditions were beginning to appear in Britain. In the 1950s and 1960s, there was large scale immigration into the country from the Caribbean, Africa, Cyprus and from the Indian sub-continent. Practically all those who came from India, Pakistan and Bangladesh practised religions other than Christianity. The result was that mosques, temples and gurdwaras began to appear in many towns and cities and many teachers found that they had in their classes children from different religious traditions.

These factors, which will be explored in more detail later in the book, led to considerable changes to the aims and content of RE in the county school and it is this developed approach to RE which was widespread in 1988 when the Education Reform Act was introduced.

## RE in the Education Reform Act

Contrary to many reports in the media at the time of the publication of the Act, the requirements on RE were not an attempt to put the educational clock back to the period of the 1944 Act but rather they reflect and enshrine in law the thought and practice which had developed in the intervening years. In its attempt to give coherence and balance to the overall curriculum, the Education Reform Act has given RE a firm, if slightly idiosyncratic place in its plans. In general, the

Education Reform Act continues the religious settlement of the 1944 Education Act but introduces some helpful clarifications and modifications.

## The basic curriculum

The Education Reform Act introduced the notion of a *basic* curriculum to which all pupils are entitled. The aim of this 'balanced and broadly based curriculum' is to promote 'the spiritual, moral, cultural, mental and physical development of pupils at the school and of society' (Section 1:2). This provides the overall framework in which RE and the 10 foundation subjects which form the National Curriculum (English, mathematics, science, technology, history, geography, music, art, physical education and in Key Stages 3 and 4 a modern foreign language plus Welsh in schools in Wales where Welsh is not spoken) are placed and it is intended that they should all make their contribution to the rounded development of individuals. None of those defined aspects of development is the preserve of any given subject. It would be a mistake to think that spiritual development is the responsibility only of RE; it would be hoped that English, science, art and music and others too would have their contribution to make.

Unlike the foundation subjects of the National Curriculum, RE has no prescribed national Attainment Targets, Programmes of Study or assessment arrangements so from this it is clear that RE has a unique place in the basic curriculum. The (then) DES Circular 3/89 expresses it:

> The special status of religious education as part of the basic curriculum but not of the National Curriculum is important. It ensures that religious education has equal standing in relation to the core and the other foundation subjects within a school's curriculum, but is not subject to nationally prescribed Attainment Targets, Programmes of Study and assessment arrangements.

This means in effect that the Secretary of State has little power over religious education. In reality the RE curriculum, rather than being national, is local — the responsibility of each local education authority.

That RE is not part of the National Curriculum seems to arise for a number of reasons. Firstly, it is no doubt partly due to the long-standing responsibility which LEAs have held for the content of RE through the Agreed Syllabus. Secondly, the existence of a conscience clause enabling parents to withdraw their children from RE would mean that some children might not be able to participate in part of the National Curriculum — and that would be odd. Thirdly, the fact that a significant number of schools are voluntary aided and can therefore teach RE according to their Trust Deeds would mean that they would be ignoring the content of the National Curriculum. It is reasonable to suspect, too, that the government feared that to reach agreement on national Programmes of Study and Attainment Targets for RE could be a very controversial process and therefore one best avoided if possible! The traditional responsibility of the LEAs for RE in their boundaries was therefore a very attractive solution. While it did solve one difficulty, it did create another. An underlying principle of the National Curriculum is that children, wherever they live in the country, should have an equal educational entitlement which should not be subject to the vagaries of the LEAs or of individual schools. Because of its essentially local character, this principle could not apply to RE. This is an issue which is still being addressed.

## The content of RE

Although the Education Reform Act deputed the RE curriculum to each LEA to devise in the form of an Agreed Syllabus it did provide a very important framework in which these syllabuses should be drawn up. This framework is contained in one sentence in the act, that all new Agreed Syllabuses must:

> reflect the fact that the religious traditions in Great Britain are in the main Christian whilst taking account of the teaching and practices of the other principal religions represented in Great Britain.

Before the implications of this sentence are examined, it is important to note the law for the first time lays down a requirement about the content of RE — that over the period of compulsory schooling pupils should have the opportunity to study a range of religious traditions. LEAs are free to draw up their Agreed Syllabuses but they must fit within this framework. This would mean, for example, that an Agreed Syllabus which included only Christianity would not be within the law and also neither would one which attempted to exclude it. This is a most definite development from the 1944 settlement and one which reflects very clearly what has been happening in the teaching of RE over the intervening years.

It is important to note that the sentence from the Act above refers to religious traditions (in the *plural*) and while it acknowledges that Christianity is the main one, it is still one among a number. The religious composition of Britain is therefore seen as *pluralist*. This has implications for the aims of RE in county schools. While it is never stated explicitly, there is the implicit assumption that RE is more concerned with developing awareness and understanding of religion and of religions than it is with any confessionalist or missionary intent.

The Act is very clear about the criteria for the selection of the religions to be included in agreed syllabuses: they should be the other principal religions represented in Great Britain. This geographical context is extremely important and has implications in two directions. Firstly, the religions to be studied are those which children will come across in moving around Great Britain. Therefore schools are not licensed to teach little known religions from the remoter parts of the world but those which are significant in this country. Secondly, each local authority is required to draw up a syllabus which reflects the fact that the religious traditions of this country are in the main Christian whilst taking account of the teaching and practices of the other principal religions represented in Great Britain. This means that all local authorities, including those in which the presence of other religious traditions is not significant numerically, must base their Agreed Syllabus upon the religious composition of Great Britain.

Although this provides extremely important guidance to LEAs in the drawing up of their Agreed Syllabuses, there are a

Does this mean that Christianity should receive a bigger time allocation than any other religion? Or should it have more than all the religions put together (i.e. 50 per cent)? Or should it have a two-thirds share of the RE curriculum time available, as recommended by the Church of England General Synod Board of Education? This is an issue upon which the government has resolutely refused to rule; it is seen to be within the remit of each local authority to make a decision according to its own local circumstances.

number of issues which are not dealt with. Nowhere does the Act specify which are 'the other principal religions represented in Great Britain'. Despite early fears that this might be an area of high controversy, these seem to have generally been accepted as Hinduism, Islam, Judaism and Sikhism and, in many cases, Buddhism as well. Nowhere does the Act give guidance upon the balance to be given to the different traditions apart from the general implication that Christianity, because of its position as the main religious tradition, should have the most.

It is interesting to note that the Model Syllabuses, produced by the Schools Curriculum and Assessment Authority (SCAA) as informal guidance to LEAs in the drawing up of an Agreed Syllabus, worked on the basis that Christianity should be awarded 50 per cent of the RE curriculum time. While these Model Syllabuses have absolutely no legal standing, they are proving to be highly influential.

It is important to note that the Act does not lay down any requirement about when different religions should be taught. Initial fears that children, even as young as five, would have to study several religions in the same year has proved to be groundless. The legal requirements are for the content of Agreed Syllabuses and these cover the teaching of RE from the age of 4 through to 16 and, in some cases, 18. Although no guidance has been given formally, again the Model Syllabuses have spread their influence. In their planning they look to two religions, Christianity and one other, as the focus in Key Stage 1 and three religions, Christianity and two others in Key Stage 2. Although these syllabuses have only an advisory function, they are again proving influential.

It is worth noting that the Education Reform Act did formally change the name of the subject from *religious instruction* to *religious education*. This was a timely change as the former term had virtually disappeared from usage. This use of the term religious education did acknowledge the broadened role of RE in the school curriculum, a broadening process which the Act itself continued.

## The role of the SACRE

The Education Reform Act requires that each LEA establish a Standing Advisory Council for Religious Education (SACRE). Its *chief function* is to

> advise the authority upon matters connected with religious worship in county schools and the religious education to be given in accordance with an agreed syllabus as the authority may refer to the Council or as the Council may see fit.  (ERA, 1988, 11.1(a))

The matters of concern referred to are likely to focus upon such items as teaching methods, the choice of teaching materials and the provision of inservice training for teachers. So as to fulfil this function the SACRE is required to publish an annual report on its activities and this report should be distributed to schools, local teacher training institutions and the Qualifications and Curriculum Authority (QCA). This report should describe the matters upon which the SACRE has advised the LEA, the advice which was given and any issues upon which the SACRE agreed to advise the LEA even though its advice was not sought. In addition to this advisory role, the SACRE does have two very specific responsibilities. Firstly, it can require the LEA to review its Agreed Syllabus. If such a requirement is made, then the LEA must constitute a Standing Conference to review the syllabus. Secondly, SACRE can consider requests from schools for a variation in the legal requirement for the act of worship. These applications would come from schools where a significant number of pupils are from religious backgrounds which are not Christian and, if SACRE approved, a school would be granted a *determination* for five years exempting it from the legal requirement to provide acts of worship which are 'wholly or mainly of a broadly Christian character', though this would not allow a school to discontinue worship. As this book is about RE rather than collective worship, this responsibility of SACRE will not be developed here but it is referred to as it is one of the few powers invested in SACRE.

The Education Reform Act is very clear about the *composition* of the SACRE. It lays down that a SACRE should be made up

In one LEA which is not noted for the multicultural or multiracial composition of its population, the 'Christian and other religious denominations' group consists of representatives from the Baptist Union, the Methodist Church, the New Churches, the Orthodox Churches, the Religious Society of Friends, the Roman Catholic Church, the Salvation Army, the United Reformed Church and representatives from Buddhism, Hinduism, Islam and Judaism. The rest of the SACRE is made up of three representatives of the Church of England, five County Councillors and representatives of the main headteachers' and teaching associations. The different size of the groupings does not matter in terms of voting and decision making as voting takes place in groups — members of SACRE disappear into four different rooms or corners of the main room and each grouping comes to its own decision.

of four representative groups (or three in Wales): Christian and other religious denominations, the Church of England (except in Wales), teachers' associations and elected councillors. It is interesting to note that these four groupings were those which the 1944 Act laid down as the constituents of the Standing Conference which was to draw up an agreed syllabus. It is important to note too that in the first named group, Christian and other denominations, there is a useful clarification in the wording. In the 1944 Act this was referred to as the 'other denominations' group for the Agreed Syllabus conference and there was always controversy as to whether this referred only to Christian denominations other than the Church of England. This new wording removes the ambiguity and now non-Christian religious traditions can belong to SACRE on equal terms with those of Christian denominations if, in the opinion of SACRE, they 'appropriately reflect the principal religious traditions of the area' (11.4(a)). This clarification is significant because it does underline the intention of the Act that RE should take account of the teaching and practices of the other principal religions represented in Great Britain.

Under new guidelines membership of the 'Christian and other religious denominations' category must reflect the relative size of the different denominations and it is up to the LEA to determine the size of membership of the different denominations within its territory, which is no easy task. Any denomination can request representation and membership and this would have to be considered by the LEA.

In addition to this membership it is also possible to coopt additional members. A particular issue has been the membership of Humanists on SACREs. Although not religious in any conventional sense, Humanists frequently have a strong interest in the approach to RE based on knowledge and understanding and have been active members of a number of SACREs. Where they are members, they have usually been offered membership under the 'Christian and other religious denominations' group. However this is no longer allowed by the Department for Education and Employment as Humanism is not strictly a religious denomination, although as a movement it does share a number of features. Humanists who are members now have to be coopted and as they do not belong to one of the four groupings, they do not have voting rights. SACREs also have the right to coopt representatives of any grant maintained schools within their area.

## Agreed Syllabuses

It has been noted already that each LEA is required to draw up an Agreed Syllabus for Religious Education within its jurisdiction, or, failing that, to adopt that of another local authority. The fact that it is called an *agreed* syllabus suggests that it must be agreed — and agreed by those who are presumed to have a special interest or concern for RE. This means in practice the general public (through their elected councillors), the teachers and the various religious traditions — the same groupings as constitute SACRE. It is sometimes claimed erroneously that it is SACRE which draws up an agreed syllabus. To draw up a syllabus the LEA must call a standing conference representing the interested parties; this is very often very similar and sometimes identical in membership to SACRE but it is not the same as SACRE — it has been set up for this one highly specific purpose.

It is laid down in the Education Reform Act that syllabuses for RE should lie within local hands. This is discussed earlier in this chapter. The freedom of each LEA in this sphere is limited to some extent by the requirement that 'all new agreed syllabuses must reflect the fact that the religious traditions in Great Britain are in the main Christian whilst taking account of the teaching and practices of the other principal religions represented in Great Britain'. Within that, however, the standing conference can decide which religions should be taught in which key stages, the key aspects of those religions which should provide the focus for the teaching and the proportions of the RE curriculum time which should be awarded to the different traditions according to the perceived local need. An agreed syllabus should contain sufficient factual content within it so that it can be a useful guide and enable any reader to gain a clear insight into its flavour. An Agreed Syllabus should form the basis of RE in county and voluntary controlled schools. Voluntary aided schools may follow their trust deeds though they can (and sometimes do) adopt the local Agreed Syllabus. Grant maintained schools are required to follow an agreed syllabus but it need not be the one of the LEA in which they are placed: they can, if they wish, adopt that of any LEA in the country. The Agreed Syllabus should provide the basic guidelines within which a school draws up its own scheme of work. Each LEA is now required to review its Agreed Syllabus every five years.

## The model syllabuses

Reference has been made several times to the Model Syllabuses. Produced by the Schools Curriculum and Assessment Authority (SCAA) in 1994, these two Model Syllabuses were set out as guidance to SACREs and Agreed Syllabus Conferences when they were devising or revising their own Agreed Syllabus. Although both were set within the same aims and objectives, they had different starting points, one working out from the religions towards the child and the other working from key religious questions and issues to the religions themselves. Although they have no legal status and are offered entirely as guidance to those involved in the revising of syllabuses, it is likely that they are already proving to be influential and may well have the effect of bringing a range of diverse Agreed Syllabuses, all originating locally, into much closer agreement.

A particular strength of the model syllabuses is the process in which they were drawn up. All of the major faiths in Britain — Christianity, Buddhism, Hinduism, Islam, Judaism and Sikhism — were each invited to set up faith working parties, backed up by consultants, to make recommendations about what they felt it was important for pupils to learn about their particular tradition. Prior to that, the subject content of the various religious traditions had been selected largely by 'outsiders', educationalists and teachers with little reference to members of these traditions.

Although there are some people who get impatient with looking to the past, it is important that RE coordinators should understand the context in which they are working. During the period since 1944 a number of approaches to RE have been in

**Faith working parties**
For the first time the faith communities were talking for themselves. These recommendations were included in the same package as the model syllabuses and are a very useful resource upon which standing conferences can draw. It is clear that the large number of newly created and revised agreed syllabuses are in fact making good use of them.

vogue and studying these is an immensely helpful way of becoming quite clear about what RE should be trying to do now. This historical survey also has a second use: RE coordinators, when they are involved in discussion with colleagues will find that some of them have become fixed in their thinking about RE at earlier points in the past. To have some understanding of these developments will enable them both to interpret attitudes expressed more clearly and also to lead thinking on more easily. This will be looked at more closely when we consider ways of working with colleagues.

# The aims of religious education

An RE coordinator was leading a staff meeting to consider how RE could best be developed and improved in his school. As a start to the session he asked his colleagues to write down on a piece of paper what they considered the aims and function of RE in a school to be. When the replies had been collected, among the fourteen of them were the following:

1   To make children into Christians I suppose. That's why I never do it. As I don't believe in God, it would be hypocritical to do so.

2   To give the children some knowledge of God, I suppose. Hardly any of my class seem to go to church or Sunday school so I suppose we are expected to fill in the gap. Just like in sex education!

3   To raise moral standards.

4   I am, as you know, a born again Christian so I see RE as an opportunity for me to share some of my experiences with the children. That's why I don't teach them about other religions as they could be a distraction from the real purpose.

5   It's a part of cultural understanding. They need to know something of religion in order to understand some of the literature they will come across, with a bit of luck, later on.

6  To foster tolerance mainly. Having some understanding of the religious beliefs, values and customs of other people is very useful in a multiracial country and world. Ignorance breeds suspicion.

7  I think it is about developing spiritual awareness. I know that the children will learn about different religions but RE should also help them to make it more personal.

8  We live in a global village and education is about helping children to make sense of it and to understand it. RE should do its bit and inform the children about beliefs and customs in different religions. That's very useful.

## Teachers' views on religious education

These responses are in some cases ambiguous — not perhaps surprisingly as the teachers were put on the spot — but they do reveal a wide range of attitudes and viewpoints and possible strategies for dealing with some of these will be considered later in the book. All of them indicate the confusion there is about the aims and purposes of RE. Views certainly do differ but it is possible to detect three broad and differing approaches often identified by writers on RE:

1  the 'confessional' approach;
2  the 'factual' approach;
3  the 'understanding religion' approach.

### The 'confessional' approach

This sees the aim of religious education as leading children into some form of Christian commitment. Responses 1, 2 and 4 above fit neatly into this approach. Underlying this approach is the assumption that Christianity is perceived to be the true way and that RE should seek to initiate pupils into it over the years of schooling. This approach has also been called the 'missionary' approach and, in practice, there is little to distinguish it from the aim of the church or the Sunday school. It is worth noting that reply 1 sees this as the aim of RE although she feels unable to support it because of her own personal beliefs.

## The 'factual' approach

This rejects completely the 'confessional' approach in its desire to lead children to some form of religious commitment. It adopts a neutral view about the truth or falsity of religions. It adopts the view that religions are an important phenomenon in the world and so children, as citizens of the world, ought to know about them. Replies 5 and 8 above would fit well into this approach.

## The 'Understanding Religion' approach

It rejects the 'confessional' approach because it does not see the aim of RE as leading children towards some form of commitment to a religious tradition (though, of course, pupils may decide to do this for themselves) but neither does it see religions only as collections of facts. Its concern is that children should *understand* religion, that is to see it from the inside, to stand in other people's shoes. The quality of empathy is therefore of central importance to this approach. In addition to this there is a conviction too that the study of religion in this way should spark off in children questions of meaning which they ask themselves. In this way, pupils not only learn *about* religion but also learn *from* it. Replies 6 and 7 would fit broadly into this approach.

## How did this variety of views come about?

It is very important that RE coordinators are very clear about the aims and purposes of RE, partly so that they can lead the development of appropriate RE in their schools and partly because they may have to spend time negotiating with colleagues their views on and attitudes towards RE. Here a short historical view might bring clarity to the different approaches. Further details of some of the legal milestones will appear in Chapters 3 and 6.

The 1944 Education Act produced a legal foundation for RE — or RI (Religious *Instruction* as it was called at that stage. In that Act, RE was made a required subject (in those times the only one) in every county school: each day should begin with an act of worship; there should be a right of withdrawal for both pupils and teachers on the grounds of conscience; and that every local education authority should formulate its own agreed syllabus for religious instruction or, failing that, adopt that of another authority. Although the Act in no place discusses the *aims* of RE, the implication of the legal requirements is that a 'confessional' approach was being implied. The very name of the subject, Religious Instruction, the daily act of worship, the right of teachers to withdraw from teaching this part of the curriculum and the parallel right of parents to withdraw their children, also on the grounds of conscience, together seemed to show that the Act assumed that children should be inducted in some way into the Christian religion. This is further confirmed by the way the compilers of the early agreed syllabuses saw their task. This extract from the Surrey syllabus of 1945 is representative of many:

> The aim of the syllabus is to secure that children attending the schools of the county . . . may gain knowledge of the common Christian faith held by their fathers for nearly two thousand years; may seek for themselves in Christianity principles which give a purpose to life and a guide to all its problems, and may find inspiration, power and courage to work for their own welfare, for that of their fellow creatures and for the growth of God's kingdom.

It is only fair to add that this approach to the teaching of religion reflected the attitudes and views of the wider society at that period. Most people identified in some way and at some level with the Christian religion. A large majority turned to the church at key times in their lives: for baptism, for marriage and for funerals even though the majority were in no sense regular churchgoers. Not all, of course, were of this view. Some groups in society such as the British Humanist Society and the National Secular Society clearly rejected any form of supernatural religion and were strongly opposed to what they saw as religious indoctrination in school but they were both very small in membership and made little headway with the vast majority of parents and teachers.

The next two decades saw changes which challenged the assumptions of this order. In the 1950s and 1960s there was immigration into Britain from the New Commonwealth on a large scale. Although the vast majority of those who came from the Caribbean were Christian in culture, most of those who came from the Indian sub-continent, from India, Pakistan and Bangladesh, to settle in Britain were Hindu, Muslim or Sikh. These groups naturally brought their religious practice with them and so over the years mosques, mandirs (Hindu temples) and gurdwaras (Sikh places of worship) began to appear. Initially worship often took place in hired halls or in converted houses but as the communities increased in size and money was raised, planning permission was sought from local authorities and purpose-built edifices began to appear in different parts of the country. These new residents had children who naturally attended the schools, primary and secondary, in their localities. This affected the religious composition of the classes and teachers in primary schools in parts of the country might well find that they had in their classes children who were Hindu, Jewish, Muslim and Sikh (and in many cases practising these religions!) alongside the usual indigenous children. Inevitably this raised questions about the appropriateness of a *confessional* approach to religious teaching and also to the restriction of the content of RE to Christianity alone. Some teachers saw no reason for adjusting their approach but many felt differently. It was in such situations as this that tentative moves were made in some multifaith schools to broaden the RE syllabus so as to include material from a range of religious traditions.

In a more general way, changes were taking place in the religious belief and practice of the population as a whole. During the 1960s there was a rapid decline in church attendance, many people felt freer about admitting religious doubt and certainly in public opinion polls on religious allegiance, the percentage of those claiming to be agnostic or atheist increased. This change was naturally reflected in the teaching profession and the number of teachers who felt it difficult to adopt a *confessionalist* approach increased.

Approaches were changing within the school also. Children in the course of their classroom work were being encouraged not to accept things merely on authority but to question, to challenge and above all to think for themselves.

The *confessional* approach to RE with its didactic approach, however well hidden by attractive presentation, did not seem to fit in here.

Despite all these changes in society and school, there were still massive and persistent demands for its continuing presence in schools. In surveys of parental views, around 90 per cent were in favour of compulsory RE in schools. Commentators put it down to many causes: guilt, a desire to off load on to the school an unpalatable part of parenthood (rather like sex education), a feeling that it might encourage good behaviour. Whatever the reasons the demand seemed to be there.

Religious education therefore continued but because of the changed and changing context of society and school, its aims began to adapt to the new situation. Confessionalism was largely unworkable but an approach which appeared attractive to many was what has been characterised as the *factual* approach. The rationale for this approach was as follows: children live in a world surrounded by the outward signs of religion: the church on the corner, the great cathedral in the nearby city, brothers and sisters baptised, aunts and uncles married, the language of the Bible permeating much of literature and thought. They need to have some awareness of this as part of their understanding of how the world works. This can be developed. Either through personal contact or through their television screens children come into contact with other religious traditions some of which have very clear views on how life ought to be lived. Children therefore need to have a some understanding of a range of religious traditions and ways of living so as to enlarge their view of the world and, hopefully, to learn greater tolerance through this knowledge. In implementing such a rationale, the teacher's role is clearly not to foster belief nor to encourage commitment to any particular religion nor even to commend a religious view as opposed to a non-religious view of life. The teacher should be neutral, providing information in such a way, appropriate to the children's age and stage, as to aid them to make more sense of the world in which they live.

On the face of it this seemed to be the ideal solution to the troubled area. It respected the plurality of society; it was seen by most people including humanists as a valuable educational activity; teachers of any religious persuasion or of none could teach it without any conflict of conscience; it was now appropriate to make statements such as 'Christians believe that Jesus is the Son of God' or 'Muslims believe that the Qu'ran is the Word of God' — factual statements about religions which any teacher could convey to any class of children — which do not have to be evaluated or examined for truth.

What had seemed the perfect solution soon seemed to many to be seriously flawed. The concern arose from the determination to be always neutral, to keep to the *facts about* religion, to be always descriptive. The danger was that pupils could learn a mass of facts about different religious traditions but come away having missed the heart. Take, for example, children making a study of the Hajj, the pilgrimage which most Muslims wish to make to Mecca at some point in their lifetime. It is quite possible for them to make a very detailed study of what Muslims *do*, even to the extent of making a frieze of the events of each day of the pilgrimage, without ever considering questions of *why* they save up all their lives to raise the air fare and *what it means to them* while they are doing it. This factual approach was in serious danger of become arid — and also of (unconsciously) presenting religious phenomena in such a way that they often appeared to children to be strange and even bizarre — because it did not focus sufficiently upon *understanding*.

It was this focus upon the *what happens* without much attention to *why does it happen* which drove other RE specialists to develop what has come to be seen as the *understanding religion* approach. There was no desire here to return to the confessional approach; they were quite clear that it is not the role of the school (except those with religious foundations) to foster a commitment to any one religious tradition in its pupils. However, they were convinced that in fairness to both children and to the religious traditions, it was important for pupils to 'get inside' religion and to have some awareness of its central questions and concerns. Hence the key term that was used was *understand*, and understanding involved empathy. There was a strong desire that children should be encouraged and helped to stand in other people's shoes and so to see things from their standpoint. Understanding in this context also involves *appreciation*. For example it is a fact that devout Muslims abstain from both food and drink during the hours of daylight during the month of Ramadan and they might think the practice impressive or strange or whatever. If, however, they are to have some understanding of it they need to have some glimmering of *why* devout Muslims fast. In this way they can begin, even if only in a small way, to enter inside a religion. In this sense it is often said that religious education should transcend the informative.

Alongside this emphasis upon looking with sensitivity at religions, and to some extent from within them, came the notion of *personal search*. This underlines the idea that children (and many adults too!) are engaged in a personal quest for meaning. Most humans at some time consider the deep, insistent questions of existence: is this all there is to life or is there more? what happens when we are dead? why be good? These questions may be asked more explicitly and in a more sophisticated form by teenagers and adults but there can be little doubt that these sorts of issues underly their questions when they are confronted by such things as grief and loss. It is such a role for RE in the development of children's understanding which has led recently, and notably in the SCAA Model Syllabuses, to the drawing of a clear distinction between two complementary focuses or aims of RE which together give it its rounded form. These two focuses are *learning about religion* and *learning from religion*. This makes absolutely clear that RE at its best both helps children to learn about religion in a sensitive and empathetic way but also seeks ways in which the children's own inner experience can be enriched. For example, the stories of the Old Testament hero, Samson, are popular in many schools, no doubt because they are stories which engage children's interest. Here the learning *about* religion would involve hearing stories about an early Jewish charismatic hero and his role in defending the faith against those who would harm it; the learning *from* religion might well help the children to consider the use and misuse of strength and reflect on this in their own dealings with others. Similarly the Jewish feast of Pesach or Passover is an increasingly popular element in RE in the primary school. It has a very powerful story dimension and its ritual and practice is rich in symbolism. To tell the children the underlying story and to reenact the Passover meal would be fulfilling the aim or focus of learning about religion and as such would be strictly speaking religious studies. For it to be religious education it would need to also think about the issue of freedom which underlies the Passover festival.

It is worth noting that RE at its best contains both focuses, learning *about* and learning *from* religion. However many non specialists teaching RE to their classes do lack confidence in their own knowledge and understanding of religion and feel especially unconfident about those areas more concerned with the learning from religion focus. Many can be carefully helped to teach about religions effectively. For many this is a major step in their professional development and most RE coordinators will wisely appreciate the success arising from their endeavours as subject managers and accept this as good RE even if it is not RE at its best! As confidence grows, then the other focus, learning from religion, will probably follow — though to push for it too soon can damage developing teaching about religions as a number of RE coordinators know to their cost!

## Spiritual and moral development

A new dimension has been opened for RE in renewed thinking about the place of spiritual and moral development in school. The Education Reform Act talks of a basic curriculum, consisting of the foundation subjects and RE, which is the entitlement of all pupils and will be provided in all maintained schools. It goes on to say that this basic curriculum 'shall be a balanced and broadly based curriculum which promotes the spiritual, moral, cultural, mental and physical development of pupils at the school and of society'. Since 1988 there has been a growing interest in these areas, especially in the spiritual and moral development and this has proved to be of considerable interest to those concerned for RE.

Spiritual development is hard to define in precise terms, partly because many people find it difficult to articulate what they mean by the term. This is further complicated by the fact that traditionally spiritual development and the broader notion of spirituality has largely been the domain of religious thought and practice. In most of the great world religions there is a basic belief in the existence of a Supreme Being who created humanity, to whom humanity can relate and whose will is the framework for human living. While this will provide a basis for spirituality for those with a religious faith, it is of less value for those without one. To be of general value to all teachers and pupils our understanding of spiritual development must be of an open process of exploring issues which are generally accepted as being related in some way to spirituality.

At root, spiritual development is concerned with helping an individual to become aware of his/her inner life. It seeks to develop an awareness that there is more to life than the physical and the material. Above all it seeks to enrich these areas which are unique to each individual. Aspects which tend to cluster around the idea of spiritual development are

- celebration
- a sense of beauty
- a sense of awe, wonder and mystery
- a sense of the transcendent
- a sense of grief, loss and transience
- a concern to know one's identity and one's relationship with the world around one
- an exploration for values by which to live
- a search for meaning and purpose in life and the responsibilities of being human (who am I and how do I relate to the world around me?)

In summary, spiritual education is concerned firstly with the individual acquiring beliefs and values within the context of that individual's overall convictions about the purpose of life and, secondly, with helping individuals to develop a basis for personal and social behaviour. In this way spiritual and moral development are closely related as, under normal circumstances, action would arise out of belief and value. It will be clear from this that spiritual and moral development cannot be the sole preserve of RE. In theory, at least, the whole school ethos expressing the values a school community holds, the acts of collective worship and all the different subjects of the school curriculum — science, English, RE, music and so on — should make their contribution.

Whereas RE is only one of many partners in spiritual and moral development it would be surprising if the subject did not have a particularly major contribution to make to spiritual and moral development because in many ways it is seeking the same ends. RE is, for example, concerned to help children to reflect upon the meaning and purpose of life and to find for themselves a faith or code by which to live. It seeks to help pupils to explore beliefs and their effect upon the lives of believers. It endeavours to introduce children to the central beliefs, values and practices of the major religious traditions which must be at least an element in a spiritual journey and to evaluate them. On the other hand it is also very important, for its own sake that spiritual and moral development should not be seen as the preserve of one subject area and that it should be perceived as overarching the whole curriculum in such a way that all subject disciplines can make their contribution.

Any attempt to provide a cognitive content to spiritual education is likely to include the following:

- **knowledge** of the central beliefs, ideas and practices of major world religions and philosophies;

- **an understanding** of how people sought to explain the universe through various myths and stories including religious, historical and scientific interpretations

- **beliefs** which are held personally and ability to give some account of them

- **behaviour and attitudes** which show relationship between belief and action

- **personal response** to questions about the purpose of life and to the experience of e.g. beauty and love or pain and suffering

Seen in this way RE has a very decided contribution to make to the development of spirituality in pupils.

## The aims of religious education

Drawing together the different strands in this discussion of the changing aim of RE, the following list is intended as a summary of the key aims of the subject which have emerged from the long debate.

RE should assist pupils to:

- acquire knowledge and understanding of the central beliefs and practices of Christianity and of the other principal religious traditions represented in Great Britain

- develop an awareness of the ways in which religious belief affects the values and behaviour of individuals and communities

- make informed judgments about religious and moral issues

- enrich their spiritual experience

- search for meaning, purpose and a faith to live by

- explore fundamental questions of life in a religious context

- reflect upon their own beliefs and values in a positive way

- develop empathy with people holding different religious beliefs and to respect and value those beliefs.

*Part three*

# Writing a school policy for RE

**Chapter 5**
Working with colleagues

**Chapter 6**
Religion and the agreed syllabus

**Chapter 7**
Writing a religious
education policy

## Chapter 5    Working with colleagues

The first step for any subject coordinator in attempting to develop any subject in a primary school is to work towards a shared vision of that subject among the staff. In a secondary school this is less of an issue as the members of the subject staff are likely to be specialists or, if not specialists, at least strongly interested in the subject. The situation in which a subject coordinator writes the policy and establishes the scheme of work on behalf of colleagues may result in a saving of staff time but it is unlikely to result in a better approach to the delivery of the subject in the classrooms; documents compiled in this way tend to end up in a filing cabinet!

## Staff attitudes to RE

While it is true to say that in many schools RE has been established and is taught in a entirely unproblematic manner, it is also fair to add that it is probably one of the more controversial subjects in the primary school curriculum. Some RE coordinators have therefore had to budget both time and energy in examining staff attitudes and understandings before the planning of the subject can proceed in an educational and rational way.

Staff do seem to be less neutral towards RE than they do towards history or PE. From my research, problems from staff which some RE coordinators have encountered focus upon:

1   their personal attitudes towards religion;
2   their understanding (or misunderstanding) of the aims
    of RE;
3   their general feeling of inadequacy about teaching RE;
4   their attitude to RE as a curriculum subject.

While the problems have been analysed in this way, there is considerable overlap between the four categories.

## I   Personal attitudes towards religion

One RE coordinator wrote:

> *I had the full range from an atheist to a born again Christian! The atheist said that her conscience could not possibly allow her to teach RE as she did not believe in God and the born again Christian said he could not possibly teach anything other than Christianity for the same reason!*

In another school some other teachers expressed negative attitudes towards Christianity because of early experiences of it. An RE coordinator wrote:

> *It is difficult to make colleagues feel comfortable about teaching parts of the syllabus particularly those connected with Christianity because of their childhood experience of it.*

In some other schools, there was among a number of the staff an absence of contact with religion in any form which lead to a lack of interest. An RE coordinator in a multiracial infants school wrote:

> *I found that I was having to overcome initial prejudice, antipathy and lack of interest.*

Sometimes teachers had formed negative attitudes to religions of the basis of superficial stereotypes. This was particularly noticeable over the popular view of Islam's attitude to the status of women.

## 2 Understanding (or misunderstanding) the aims of RE

There was much evidence in the research of considerable misunderstanding of the aims and purposes of RE. There was quite a widespread view among teachers, surprising perhaps after so long, that the aim of RE, to use the technical term, is confessional, i.e. it is attempting to induct children into a belief system. This is borne out by some of the quotations above. The atheist teacher, for example, whose conscience will not let her teach RE is implying that she sees the objective of RE being to teach children to accept a religious faith. One RE coordinator summed up the situation very succinctly:

❛ *My great initial problem was to sort out the misunderstanding of the staff over teaching RE and evangelism.*

## 3 General feeling of inadequacy about teaching RE

Many RE coordinators noted a general feeling of inadequacy about teaching RE among the staff of their schools, in some cases of feeling threatened by it. This inadequacy arose partly out of scant knowledge of religions. As one RE coordinator put it:

❛ *We simply do not know enough information. Not many staff know how to teach it.*

This feeling of inadequacy was in some cases more finely focused. Again, an RE coordinator wrote:

❛ *There is an anxiety in my school, which I also share, of 'treading on the toes' of religious faiths, of offending without meaning to, or even realising.*

This concern was certainly more marked in schools with a multifaith composition but there was still a feeling in a wider number of schools that religion is an area of special significance to groups of people and so needs to be respected.

More serious was a weakness that a number of RE coordinators noted in some of their colleagues: blindness to the underlying concerns of religion.

❛ *My biggest problem was getting some of the staff to teach a subject they have no empathy with.*

❛ *The most difficult issue with one or two colleagues is a lack of spiritual awareness.*

Whereas this was not widespread, it did create problems for RE coordinators in some schools.

## 4 Attitudes to RE as a curriculum subject

Attitudes to RE in the curriculum varied considerably and certainly many coordinators found in the early stages of developing the subject that many staff felt:

❛ *RE is less important than many other parts of the curriculum. In many ways I cannot see its value.*

❛ *The National Curriculum demands so much that I have neither the time or the energy to devote to RE. If it is so important, why is it not placed firmly in the National Curriculum?*

❛ *In a busy week the first thing that will be squeezed out is RE.*

❛ *Some of the staff (by no means all, thank goodness) see RE as an obstacle to learning instead of an enlargement of the children's experience.*

In many cases these attitudes obtained before the development of RE in the school and the increased understanding of the nature of RE did result in a modification of views. However, there were other views quite widely expressed and these related mainly to the content of the RE curriculum:

❛ *In our school (an infant school) there is a widespread feeling among staff that by teaching a range of religions we succeed only in confusing our pupils. Much better, we think, to concentrate on Christianity. The children have enough difficulty understanding that without bringing in others. We feel it is much better to leave the other religions until the children are older.*

*Our school (a junior school) has a school population which is mainly Hindu and Sikh. We feel that it would be more appropriate to focus on these as they are the children' religions — and they mean a lot to them.*

These are the main issues which RE coordinators in the research identified as those which they had to deal with when they began the process of developing RE in their schools.

## Developing the shared vision

If a shared vision is to be developed it is very important that sufficient time is given for staff to talk through issues which affect them. While this is important for all subjects it is especially so for RE as there are probably more issues which need to be resolved before it is realistic to proceed to compiling a commonly held RE policy. Many RE coordinators have made the point that it is important to have a span of time to get to grips with the sort of issues described above. A day closure for inservice purposes devoted to RE would be the best solution but, failing this, a half day is the minimum. Once the staff has had the opportunity to come to some common understanding about the nature of RE, then shorter after-school or lunch-time sessions which deal with agreeing the policy and planning the scheme of work will probably be adequate. It is understandable that headteachers, aware of how much planning and reviewing has to be done by the staff across the whole curriculum, may be tempted to leave as little time as they consider reasonable but in the case of RE there is no short cut. If RE is to be established satisfactorily staff members do need to have the opportunity to share attitudes and concerns and to understand how RE can be an educational activity.

## Key features found in schools where RE is successful

Schools, of course, differ widely and a visitor only has to enter a school to sense immediately something of its ethos. In the same way the success of RE is also variable but for it to be successful in a school there do seem normally to be a number of factors present which make this possible.

Firstly, there normally needs to be a headteacher who is prepared to implement the law with regard to RE and to see that the opportunities are provided for RE to flourish. This could, of course, be said of all manner of subjects in the curriculum.

This is not calling for any special treatment for RE but merely expecting headteachers to implement the law which states that the basic curriculum (which includes RE) is compulsory in school, that RE should be taught according to the local agreed syllabus and that it should, according to the recommendation in the Dearing Report, be allocated 5 per cent of curriculum time. In other words, it is reasonable to expect that in their role as managers, headteachers will ensure that RE is accorded at least the same status as the non-core foundation subjects — in terms of money to buy resources, of staff development time, of opportunities for monitoring the subject in the school and of supporting members of staff in the planning and delivery of the subject.

As RE coordinator you need to believe in the importance of the subject in school and expect parity with other non-core subjects. This could, of course, be said of the history or geography coordinator too, but it is perhaps necessary for the RE coordinator to be more available as a support to other colleagues because RE is an area in which many teachers do feel in need of extra special support.

Schools in which RE is successful seem to have a shared understanding of what the teaching of RE trying to achieve. There is usually an RE policy which is understood and agreed by the staff as a whole and a scheme of work which all follow. There are also resources to support the teaching in the classroom.

Below are two case studies which describe how two recently appointed RE coordinators set about the task of developing RE in their schools. The first is set in a junior school with an enthusiastic young coordinator working with a staff that is not ill-disposed to RE but which has little coherent teaching of the subject. The second is set in a primary school in which a long established teacher volunteers to add RE coordination to the rest of her responsibilities to work with her headteacher to develop RE among a staff who are initially resistant to such a move.

## Case study 1

Wealdview Junior School is a three form entry junior school in south-east England, serving a socially mixed area. It is situated on the edge of a council estate but its natural catchment area stretches over into a country area which contains large private properties. Although there is a significant Muslim population in the area, very few of those children come to Wealdview; most of the pupils are of white Christian origin although there are a few Hindu children whose families live on the estate and there are some Sikh children whose families run local shops.

The RE coordinator has been at the school since she began teaching and is now in her fifth year. Initially she held the PE coordinatorship. She undertook her training at a college which had a strong church connection and opted to take RE as one of a range of subsidiary subjects. She had always on her teaching practices set aside time within RE to look at different religions but when she came to the school the then headteacher informed her very clearly that this approach was not adopted at the school! RE was not a strong subject in the school's curriculum: there was a dimly remembered RE policy but no coordinator for the subject and what RE was done was left to individual teachers. Some neglected to teach it at all while others focused exclusively upon Christianity.

It was when a new headteacher was appointed to the school that RE became a more central focus for curriculum development. The new headteacher invited the county RE adviser to a staff meeting at the school. His objective was to raise the level of awareness of what RE should be and to this end he brought in artefacts to show and talked about changing aims and approaches in the subject. This session had quite an impact on the staff as a whole. It made teachers aware of the type of work they should be doing but, because they had never approached RE in that way before, they had little idea of how to start. It was at this point that the RE coordinator offered to take on the responsibility, provided she could be relieved of her PE brief.

She assumed the RE mantle at Easter time and was very concerned to capitalise on the new enthusiasm in case it waned. There were still objections to be countered. Some staff thought that anything not in the National Curriculum was optional. This had to be disabused and it was clearly pointed out that RE was firmly in the basic curriculum and as such was compulsory. Others understood that RE was required by the Education Reform Act to be 'mainly and broadly Christian'. Here again there was a misunderstanding — this refers to collective worship in school which is not the same as RE. Others were concerned about the demands made on time by all the competing demands of the curriculum. The RE coordinator agreed to attempt to meet this at the planning stage.

The RE coordinator perceived immediately that the main obstacle in the way of developing RE in the school was a lack of staff confidence and that lack of confidence related to both approaches to teaching RE and to staff knowledge about religion. She felt that the best way to encourage this confidence to grow was to get teachers teaching it however basic that teaching might be. She therefore decided to do adopt three approaches intended to foster a feeling of teacher security. Firstly, she decided to devise her own scheme of work which would be basic and straightforward and one which staff could teach; secondly, she decided to invest as much as she could in resources, especially artefacts, because these were items which provided pegs on which staff could hang their RE teaching; thirdly she decided to spend time talking to each year group team, suggesting ways in which their RE teaching could fit best with their broad overall plans.

An example of this is the Year 6 topic on Communication and Books. Here there is a natural extension to an appropriate RE sub-topic, Sacred Books. The RE coordinator discussed with the teaching team the possibilities of developing this, beginning with the Bible and considering how it evolved, how it was translated, the different types of books within it and how it is used within the Christian community. From this the topic moves on to consider the sacred books of other religions such as the Tenakh (the Jewish Bible) and the Qu 'ran. There are artefacts to back these up; there is, for example, a copy of the Qu 'ran and a stand for it. The RE coordinator discusses with the teachers activities which they could undertake and provides them with background information both orally and through books which she has provided as staff resources. Often she uses her hour per week coordinator's time to teach alongside staff who are less confident in RE. In this way she has set the teachers off on the path of teaching RE and with this has come greater confidence. As teachers become more confident, so they are able to develop their own RE teaching and to devise their own activities.

The RE coordinator is pleased with the way RE is developing in the school in the space of one year. It has not been without cost to her. She has had to work hard to extend her own knowledge and understanding of different religious traditions and has had to spend many break times explaining the significance and usage of different artefacts! She was even willing to produce worksheets. She feels that the time is now ripe to review the first simple scheme of work and to develop it into something which is more demanding. It will be time to introduce more visits to religious places and to bring speakers from different faith communities into the school. After that, once the staff is happy with the scheme of work, it will be time to revisit the dimly remembered RE policy document. The RE coordinator believes strongly that a curriculum policy should be the produced by the whole staff. Had the staff members not been involved in teaching RE they would not have had sufficient understanding about the subject to have written the policy. So here it was logical for the scheme of work to precede the policy.

---

The key features of this case study seem to be:
- an initial event with the staff to raise awareness
- a very keen and committed RE coordinator
- a staff who on the whole were well disposed to RE
- a recognition of the need to build the self confidence of the staff
- the importance of starting from where the teachers are

- a willingness to start simply and to move slowly
- the planned availability of resources, especially artefacts
- a recognition of the importance of 'spoon feeding' staff in the early stages of working
- the willingness of the RE coordinator to be a constant support
- a clear plan to help staff to continue to develop their expertise in the subject
- to provide an opportunity for the teachers to crystallise their understanding of RE in the composing of the RE policy document

## Case study 2

Romans County Primary School is a one form entry school serving just over 200 children aged 4–11 years in a midlands county. The staff consists of eight full-time teachers including the headteacher along with a part-time SENCO. The RE Coordinator who is also the English coordinator is one of the longer serving members of staff. She volunteered to lead RE as well, partly because of an interest in religion and partly because she saw the possibility of using her beloved drama in the subject.

Although she felt fairly confident about teaching Christianity she was aware of the faintness of her knowledge of other world faiths so she enrolled on a part-time diploma course in RE at the local university. This she claims was invaluable in providing her with a thorough understanding of the aims and purposes of RE as well as a knowledge of some of the other world faiths. This knowledge also gave her *confidence* in developing the subject in school and in dealing with the issues which her colleagues raised.

Up to this time RE had been a weak area in the curriculum. There were two copies of the County Agreed Syllabus in the staffroom and what RE was taught was left to the judgment of individual classteachers. Some classteachers did provide some RE teaching in their classrooms but what was undertaken was neither coherent nor planned and when it was taught it was usually seen as the handmaid of the class topic — and then it almost invariably reflected Christianity.

The headteacher was keen to develop and improve the teaching of RE partly because it was, as he put it, part of the 'entitlement' curriculum and partly because he was aware that it would be inspected in the next school inspection! He was therefore prepared to give RE the same allocation of staff training time and the same funding as he provided for history and geography.

The RE coordinator, in consultation with the headteacher, decided that the first task was to undertake an audit of what was already happening in the school in terms of RE. As a long established member of staff, she had a shrewd idea already of what was taking place but she also wanted a more formal mechanism for eliciting the information. Members of staff were therefore asked to complete a simple questionnaire in preparation for a staff meeting which was being set up as the first stage of creating an RE policy for the school. From both the informal awareness and the formal findings of the questionnaire it was clear that every class did some explicit RE at Christmas time. Apart from this, it was also clear that in Key Stage 1 all three classes did only 'implicit' RE based on caring themes such as friends, families, pets and so on, in most ways indistinguishable from Personal and Social Education but appearing on the timetable as RE. Year 3 did lots of Bible stories from both Old and New Testaments, Years 4 and 5 did very little, if any, RE additional to Christmas, and Year 6 was the RE coordinator's class.

In the first staff meeting, which lasted, as planned, for one hour and a quarter, there was considerable discussion in justification of the status quo. The teachers in Key Stage 1 argued that they followed the appropriate approach to RE with young children, that children had great difficulty in understanding the concepts of religion which at that age was largely meaningless to them and that the idea of adding additional religion would merely compound the problem. Was this a genuine reason or an excuse? The teacher in Year 3 was a keen member of an evangelical church and felt it was her duty to give the pupils some insight into the nature of Christianity. She was not happy teaching other religions because she suspected personally that they might be 'in error'. The teacher with Year 4 was not in the least interested in religion and really could not see the point of spending precious time in a crowded timetable on RE. The teacher in

Year 5 claimed that as a non-believer it would be hypocritical for him to teach RE which was the reason why he didn't. In addition it became clear that there was a widespread ignorance of world religions in general which in turn led to a lack of confidence in teaching the subject. The mood of the staff meeting had been completely unaggressive but the RE coordinator went home with the knowledge that she had a considerable task ahead of her.

Analysing the meeting later it seemed that there were a number of key issues which would have to be addressed:

- the nature of RE — clearly the Year 3 and Year 5 teachers saw RE in confessional terms;
- the nature of religion — clearly the Key Stage 1 teachers were offering a very narrow opportunity to their pupils; the RE coordinator suspected that the teachers' justification was more a rationalisation than a reason;
- the entitlement of children to RE — clearly the Year 4 teacher was improperly placing her own feelings against national policy as also were all the other teachers to some extent;
- the lack of confidence arising out of lack of knowledge — this was clearly widespread across the teachers.

The RE coordinator knew that all of the above issues would have to be addressed but she also felt that she needed to develop some interest in the subject which would provide a proper motivation for the teachers to train themselves to teach RE well. She herself had always found RE enjoyable to teach and she knew that her pupils had always relished it too. To this end she set up a staff INSET day to be directed by an outside leader. The teachers began the day in a slightly apprehensive mood. On entering the room the leader placed them in three groups of three (the headteacher and the SENCO were included) each with its own table and then spent no more than two minutes explaining what religious artefacts are. He then produced a box of assorted artefacts for each table and set the teachers the task of using detective skills to guess what their purpose was, to group them according to perceived use and to identify to which religious tradition they belonged. The effect of this practical activity was quite amazing. Teachers predicted, disagreed, argued but above all *enjoyed* the activity.

After the reporting back the leader went through the artefacts and talked about them as he went so that all could judge how perceptive they had been. The outcome of this session was twofold: firstly, teachers had discovered that RE could be enthralling and secondly, as a result of the session, they had learned so much about religion!

This change of mood eased the rest of the day considerably. The leader looked closely at the nature of religion using Ninian Smart's dimensions and drawing upon the earlier work on artefacts. He also began to show how explicit religious material such as stories, festivals and ceremonies such as baptism could be well within the orbit of Key Stage 1. This did offer a broader view to the teachers in Key Stage 1 and provide them with some suggestions for providing a more balanced RE programme.

Another hour in the day's programme dealt with requirements about RE laid out in the 1988 Education Reform Act and also with developments since then. It was emphasised that teachers had the right to withdraw from the teaching of RE on the grounds of conscience but if any intended to do this it was their responsibility to do this formally so that arrangements could be made for the children to receive their entitlement. The leader also spent time explaining the aims and purposes of RE, emphasising especially its role in helping children to gain a sympathetic understanding of religious positions and activities and to begin to develop a personal view of the great issues of life. This section did have an impact upon the teachers in Key Stage 2.

This INSET day was the real beginning of the process of refurbishing RE in the school. It did not wave a magic wand over the staff and turn each member overnight into an enthusiastic and committed RE teacher. What it did do was to show them that RE could be interesting and enjoyable and that it did have a contribution to make to the education of children. There was still much talking to do but a positive start had been made.

An issue which would have to be resolved was the level of teachers' religious knowledge and understanding. Here the head agreed to fund a staff visit (afternoon and early evening) to an area of ethnic minority settlement so that all the teachers could visit a Hindu mandir, a Sikh gurdwara and a mosque. This again fanned interest through providing first hand experience and made a considerable difference to the RE coordinator's work.

The staff as a whole was quite prepared to entrust the writing of the RE policy to the RE coordinator but she very sensibly refused as she felt that all must have some involvement if RE was to be fully understood. Because of the teachers' continuing lack of confidence in their own knowledge and understanding of religions, it was conceded that initially the school would restrict itself to teaching from two religions, Christianity and one other. The staff opted overwhelmingly for Islam. The RE coordinator undertook to resource Christianity and Islam with a supply of information books and artefacts and to make herself a living and walking fount of information upon which they could draw. This concession was made on the understanding that once the teachers had begun to feel confident with these two then a third one would be added.

---

The key features of this case study seem to be:
- a keen and highly experienced teacher who volunteered to be the RE coordinator
- a headteacher who was prepared to support with staff inservice time and some outlay of financial resources
- a staff on the whole not well disposed to RE
- bringing in an 'expert' leader from outside who planned a day to meet the identified staff concerns
- the attempt to encourage motivation through involving the teachers in interesting and enjoyable RE activities
- arranging a staff visit to religious centres to enhance knowledge and understanding and to develop motivation
- to agree to making a simple start with only two religions
- the building up of suitable resources to support the two religions taught
- the willingness of the RE coordinator to be a constant support
- the insistence of the RE coordinator that the policy must be a product of the whole staff.

## Chapter 6

Religion and the agreed syllabus

It is essential that any school programme for RE should reflect and present a balanced account of religion. In very many primary schools, RE is still in danger of being taught in a haphazard way. Frequently it consists of a series of stories about Jesus, following a theme such as the miracles of Jesus, or it focuses upon a festival such as Christmas or Divali, or it is an aspect of a topic such as water or transport. For pupils to have a coherent experience of religion it is important that RE coordinators should have a clear view of the *breadth* of the activity designated 'religion.' This will give them a deeper understanding of the rationale behind the local agreed syllabus with which they are confronted, therefore, it seems appropriate to provide a broad basis of knowledge from which RE coordinators can work.

These seven dimensions of religion could form the basis for Programmes of Study and Attainment Targets for RE.

## Religion as a seven-dimensional activity

There is a considerable amount of activity going on in the world which is commonly described as 'religious'. Many, many millions of people claim to belong to one religion or another and over most of the world there is extensive evidence of religious practice and devotion. To observe both closely and widely that phenomenon called religion in its various forms and then to attempt to describe it is likely to give a helpful picture of religion for our purposes. This was the approach adopted by Ninian Smart and the result of his analysis of his observations was summarised firstly in his six dimensions of religion (Smart, 1968) and more recently (Smart, 1989) in his seven dimensions of religion. There is nothing sacrosanct about Smart's account of religion; others might well do it differently. It is, however, described here because many have found it to be a very helpful tool in understanding religion, so helpful, in fact, that it has been used as the basis for a number of approaches to religious education.

**Smart's seven dimensions of religion are:**
the practical and ritual dimension;
the experiential and emotional dimension;
the narrative and mythic dimension;
the doctrinal and philosophical dimension;
the ethical and legal dimension;
the social and institutional dimension;
the material dimension.

Although Smart has identified these seven dimensions, he would still see a religion as a unity. Although the dimensions can each be identified and studied separately, they are all facets of the same activity and, as such, are interrelated and interconnected indissolubly and RE coordinators might find the following exposition of these dimensions of some help in their quest to extend their own subject knowledge.

## The practical and ritual dimension

The practical and ritual dimension encompasses all those actions and activities which worshippers do in the practice of their religion. It ranges from the closing of the eyes in prayer to the once-in-a-lifetime pilgrimage to a holy place. It includes services, festivals, ceremonies, customs, traditions, clothing, symbols. In many ways this dimension is the shop window of a religion. Illustrations of what would come under the heading

Very often the rituals are enactments of the stories. In Judaism an historical event of tremendous significance is the Exodus when the Jews saw the hand of God in rescuing them from their slavery in Egypt. The Passover meal, celebrated annually in the home, re-enacts this great act of salvation and, during the course of the meal, the ancient story is recounted and made real in the present. On Good Friday Christian pilgrims in Jerusalem regularly retread the Via Dolorosa, the way of sorrow, the path which Christ trod on the way to his crucifixion. As they stop at the various stations of the cross they remember the times that Christ stopped on that journey. The ritual re-enacts the stories and so makes it real and alive to the pilgrims.

of the practical and ritual dimension are: the celebration of festivals: Divali, Christmas, Passover, Edi-ul-Fitr, and so on; acts of worship: the Eucharist in Christianity, the daily prayers in Islam, the worship of the synagogue and the temple; the making of pilgrimage to holy places such as Lourdes, Makkah, Jerusalem, Varanasi. Customs and postures in worship, distinctive forms of dress, initiation rites and many, many other matters would be classified in this dimension.

It is important not to be misled by the use of the word *ritual*. In every day speech this has come to be used in the pejorative sense of something which is empty and mechanical, devoid now of any real meaning or significance. While it is certainly true that religious ritual acts can, like all other acts, degenerate into this state, in this context ritual is merely a neutral descriptive term for the activities in a religion which are significant to its followers. Rituals provide the framework both for sustaining and deepening the worshipper's faith.

The practical and ritual dimension is very closely related to the narrative and mythic dimension (i.e. the stories).

## The experiential and emotional dimension

At the core of religion is *feeling* and the experiential and emotional dimension bears witness to this. Most, if not all, religious believers would claim that at the centre of their religion is an experience, however fleeting or dim, of the divine. The religious traditions record significant examples: Moses on Mount Horeb when he saw the burning bush, Isaiah of Jerusalem in the temple, St Paul on the road to Damascus, Muhammad in the caves around Makkah, Arjuna as recorded in the Bhagavad Gita. In most religions too, there are mystical traditions in which individuals claim to have had direct and searing experience of the divine. There are also the startling feelings of awe and wonder, what Rudolph Otto described as the 'numinous', in the face of the majesty and wonder of creation which people, and not only believers, experience at certain moments and which are essential to an understanding of the religious impulse.

The experience of most religious believers can be described in much less dramatic and much more homely ways — but none the less significant to them for that. This could be described as a feeling of being in tune with creation, a feeling of being given inner strength in times of difficulty, a feeling as John Wesley expressed it, of the heart at times being strangely warmed.

This dimension can be described as being the core of religion. This is because it provides the motivation for the believer and makes the practice of religion worthwhile. It is this experience, this feeling, which makes the performing of the rituals a living and satisfying experience rather than a participation in an historical curiosity; it brings the stories to life; it encourages the believer to follow the often difficult ethical path which the religion lays before its adherents; it gives the reason for believers to commit themselves to the credal statements. It is this dimension which is the inner heart of religion.

## The narrative and mythic dimension

This dimension, in simple terms the 'story' dimension, is the means of conveying the teaching of a religion through stories, poems, legends, hymns and so on. Every religion has a mass of stories which has become one of its essential elements. These stories are of different kinds. Some will be based on historical events, some are about a time before history, some are about the future, some are about significant people within the religious tradition.

Significant stories in Christianity involve 'heroes' of the Christian faith, accounts of men and women who have lived out their Christian vocation within their own era.

Most religions have scriptures, sacred writings, which are key documents, written down in many cases after a long period of oral transmission. These scriptures are recognized by the religious community as having authority. Many would see these scriptures as in some sense inspired by God. The Bible, as the sacred book of the Christian religion, is a collection of stories, history (though history with a special interpretation),

In Christianity, for example, crucial stories centre around the life, death and resurrection of Jesus Christ as recorded in the Gospels.

Such 'heroes' who could be drawn from the full sweep of Christian history might include the Apostles, St Augustine, St Benedict, St Francis of Assisi, St Teresa of Avila, Martin Luther, Father Damien, St Maximilian Kilbe and, in our own age, Mother Teresa of Calcutta, Helder Camara of Recife and many, many more. In fact, there are so many significant figures that each individual will have his or her own list! In Islam the key stories centre round the life of the Prophet and the message he delivered. Also of great importance are the accounts of the other prophets from Adam down to Muhammad and the story of the tremendous growth of Islam both in its early years and in the present age.

prophecy, letters, law, poetry and gospels which gained authority within the early church and was finally accepted by the Church as canonical. Most Christians accept the central authority of the Bible and would acknowledge that it is divinely inspired, though they might interpret this in different ways.

Islam, Sikhism and Judaism also acknowledge one sacred book, the Qu'ran, the Guru Granth Sahib and the Jewish Scriptures respectively and, of course, Christianity and Islam both draw very heavily upon the Jewish tradition. Hinduism is different in that it has a number of sacred books, which it divides into two categories: the *scruti* — that is, scriptures directly inspired by God (the Vedas, the Brahmanas and the Upanishads) and the *dmriti* — that is, books by holy men or prophets (Epics, Puranas, the Bhagavad Gita). The most popular of the Hindu scriptures is the Bhagavad Gita.

As RE coordinator it may help if you bear in mind that in his earlier account of the six dimensions of religion, Smart (1968) called this dimension the mythological dimension, and although the title has now been adjusted, writers often use the term 'myth' for these stories. This can be unhelpful as in everyday usage the word 'myth' means an untrue story. However, in its more technical sense, the term derives from the Greek *muthos*, which means, literally, 'story'. To describe the sacred stories of the world's religions as mythological is not to pass any judgment upon their truth. The term is completely neutral.

## The doctrinal and philosophical dimension

All major religions have a set of doctrines or beliefs which form part of its foundation. In Christianity, the doctrinal dimension is expressed in the creeds which have been defined in church councils in the early centuries of the church's existence. The most frequently used creed is the Nicene Creed which focuses upon two basic doctrines: the Trinity (the belief in one God in three persons, Father, Son and Holy Spirit) and the Incarnation (the entry of God into humanity in the person of Jesus Christ). This creed is recited each Sunday when the

Eucharist is celebrated and the worshippers present subscribe to it. Within Judaism there is great stress upon the oneness of God and in his loving kindness. In Hinduism there is a central belief in Brahman, the life force, and in the millions of gods who are but manifestations of the 'One'. Within Islam there is a strict emphasis upon the uniqueness of God. These doctrines are binding upon the believer. Five times each day the Muslim professes 'There is no God but Allah and Muhammad is His prophet' and this frequency of recitation is a binding rule of Islam.

Just as the ritual dimension draws upon the narrative dimension and in turn brings it to life in the experience of the believer, so the doctrinal dimension arises from the stories and proceeds to systematize and codify them. In the Christian tradition the doctrines of the Trinity and of the Incarnation, referred to earlier, were attempts by the church to explore the relationship of Jesus, who in the narratives appears to be in some sense God (which conviction seemed to be reflected in the experience of the first Christians), with the monotheism of the Jewish faith in which they had been raised. The very early Christian affirmation was 'Jesus is Lord'. But what exactly did this mean? The desire for an intellectual statement of belief, allied with a desire to refute interpretations which seemed to be erroneous, led to an increased concern to clarify formal beliefs. And so the creeds arose.

There will inevitably be different levels of understanding between educated and simple followers and there will be different interpretations of the doctrines, some being more literal or more symbolic than others.

## The ethical and legal dimension

All religions give guidance to their followers on how to conduct themselves in this world. Judaism, for example, has always placed great emphasis upon the Torah, the Law, revealed by God and required of all those who follow the tradition. The Torah consists of a vast array

The doctrinal and philosophical dimension of any religion is an attempt to give greater substance and clarity to the beliefs which are enshrined within its traditions.

of legal requirements of which the best known are the Ten Commandments. The importance of the Torah is demonstrated in the ritual dimension by a Jewish boy's bar mitzvah (and in liberal or reform Jewish circles also by a Jewish girl's bat mitzvah). When a Jewish boy reaches 13, he comes of age and demonstrates this by reading from the Torah in the synagogue. By so doing he becomes bar mitzvah (literally, son of the Law) and so takes upon himself the responsibility of keeping the Law and so of living by it. Christianity has tended to replace a system of legal requirements with a central ethical attitude, sometimes called the law of love: 'You shall love the Lord your god and your neighbour as yourself'. This ethical notion is deeply rooted in the doctrinal dimension where the Godhead is proclaimed as a Trinity of three persons co-existing in love. Christians look to the stories of Jesus as an example for living and there they see him giving his life to the world out of love.

In the modern world religions are being challenged to develop and express ethical attitudes towards such issues as ecology and nuclear weapons. Although the problems are new the process is not, as religions have always had the responsibility of applying their ethical principles to the issues of the day and as RE coordinator you must be sensitive regarding the introduction of these aspects of religion, perhaps seeking guidance from someone such as the LEA RE adviser.

## The social and institutional dimension

The social dimension of religion is concerned with the expression of that religion in society or how, as Smart puts it, it is incarnated. Every religion expresses itself in human society and all religions assume a corporate nature. In Judaism, for example, it is important to look closely at the organization of the synagogue and its relationship to the home and family which have a very special place in the Jewish tradition. In Christianity, the Church, as the body of the faithful, is of central importance and within that the role of the bishop in the unity of the church and of the priest in the work of the individual parishes. Religious communities with their monks and nuns are highly significant in most religions and there are also the gurus, the prophets and the seers, the charismatic people who are highly influential in religious movements (and often perceived by those in a formal position in the religious structure to be a nuisance!) but who are not part of the formal structure of the religion. It would include also social structures emanating from a religion such as the caste system within Hinduism.

There is another aspect to this dimension. Many religions have a vision of how human society should be organised and how people ought to view each other and the world in which they live. In Christianity, for example, as in other religions, there is a strong belief that men and women are all brothers and sisters and children of God. There have therefore been movements within Christianity to resist oppression because it offends against this vision, for example, Wilberforce to free the slaves, Martin Luther King for equal rights for black people and Trevor Huddeston against apartheid.

## The material dimension

This is the seventh dimension of religion, the one which Smart added to his original six. As the social and institutional dimension indicates how religions are incarnated in institutions and in human society, so the material dimension shows how they are incarnated in *material* form. These incarnations in material form can be either in the form of human creations — buildings or works of art — or in natural phenomena upon which special significance has been placed by religion traditions. Although puritanical groups show suspicion of such forms of outward symbolism, for most people in most religions they have been and are powerful and evocative aids in the approach to God. A visit to the cathedral of the Assumption of the Virgin in Smolensk on its patronal festival with the huge dimensions of the building, the majesty and beauty of the icons in the iconastasis and the haunting quality of the music provides an arresting example of the material dimension.

It is possible to name other analyses of religion but Ninian Smart's is probably as good as any and better than most. It highlights the seven dimensions and this shows clearly how *broadly based* an activity religion is. It demonstrates too a *balanced* understanding of religions.

In addition to these human creations, which are present and powerful in all religious traditions, there are the natural phenomena which again are powerful evocations of the divine. The sacred River Ganges, Ayers Rock, Mount Sinai are all holy ground to different religious traditions. Sometimes these sacred places merge with the human creations described above. Supreme examples of these are the city of Jerusalem, Varanasi, Lourdes, Amritsar and Makkah.

The material dimension has very clear links with the ritual dimension which in many cases is a response to it. Christian pilgrims to Jerusalem will, as a response to the sacredness of the place, retrace the steps of Jesus on his journey from his trial to his crucifixion: the ritual dimension is responding to the material dimension.

## The agreed syllabus

Every local education authority is required to draw up an agreed syllabus of religious education or, failing that, to adopt the syllabus of another authority and as religious education coordinator you will need to be aware of the syllabus adopted by your LEA. Details of how an agreed syllabus is drawn up and approved can be found in Chapter 3.

Although the National Curriculum subjects all have a nationally laid down content, the 1988 legislation decreed that RE should continue with its local, as opposed to national, associations. Because of this it would be technically possible for there to be as many widely differing agreed syllabuses as there are local education authorities. This is fortunately not the case because of:

■ the work of Ninian Smart just described, which sees religion as a complex activity which people engage in rather than as an historical study, has been very influential in RE thinking;

■ the 1988 Education Reform Act laid down certain requirements as to content;

■ the model syllabuses, which have no legal status but have provided a very helpful way of implementing the requirements of the 1988 Education Reform Act, have been influential with standing conferences on RE;

■ the movement away from a confessional approach to the teaching of RE to one which emphasises knowledge and understanding.

Anyone who doubts this development has only to look back to the agreed syllabuses which appeared in the 1940s and 1950s with their focus upon the Bible almost as the text book and to compare them with any recent syllabus.

Although agreed syllabuses were each developed in their own local regions, they do share the same rationale for RE which has been in the process of development over a quarter of a century or more. Because they share the same rationale, they have a number of common features among which are the following:

■ most have two Attainment Targets, one cognitive (learning *about* religion) and one affective (learning *from* religion);

■ there is a very clear concern that pupils' experience of RE should be balanced, progressive and coherent;

■ there is a strong desire to identify levels of attainment and most recent syllabuses have laid out end of key stage indications of attainment;

■ there is an emphasis upon the dimensions of religion with a focus upon those which are more accessible to different age groups;

■ there is a movement to greater degrees of prescription especially at Key Stages 1 and 2;

■ there is an emphasis upon first hand experience especially with regard to visits to places of worship, visits from members of faith communities and the use of artefacts;

■ there is an increasing practice of recommending which religions should be studied at which stage. In this there seems to be a preference (unless local conditions make other choices more appropriate) for Christianity and Judaism in Key Stage 1 and Christianity, Hinduism and Islam in Key Stage 2;

■ there is usually an encouragement to schools to consider how best their RE can be taught: within general topics, as a mini-topic, as a discrete subject or as part of PSHE/Circle time.

## Issues for discussion

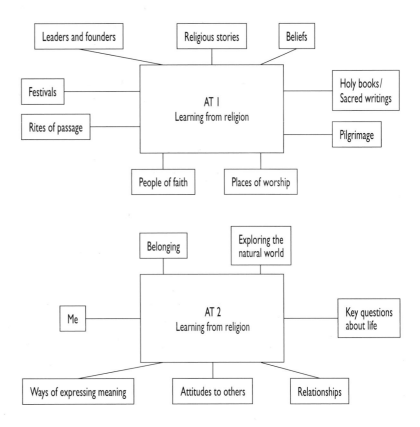

On this map of an agreed syllabus, which reflects in a broad sense the approach of most recent syllabuses, the key areas for teaching are laid out. To present it in this way can be helpful to you in your role as RE subject leader as it gives at a glance a view of what should constitute a balanced and coherent RE programme over a key stage. It initially highlights the twin areas of the 'knowledge and understanding of religion' on the one hand and the area of 'meaning' on the other, both of which should be central to any planning of RE in a school. Then it indicates important areas within those two Attainment Targets. Such a layout can be a very useful quick check by an RE coordinator for balance across a key stage. Conversely, those Key Stage 1 teachers whose RE consists only of the care of pets could see at a glance how inadequate their approach is!

## Learning about and learning from religion

This form of words which came to prominence in the model syllabuses has proved to be a very useful clarification in thinking about RE. It distinguishes very clearly between that part of RE which seeks to induct pupils into a knowledge of a range of religions linked with a sympathetic and empathetic understanding of what people within them believe and do from that part which seeks to foster in pupils a conscious attempt to pursue questions of meaning (why I am here? is there any purpose? why be good? what do good and bad mean? how should I relate to other people? and so on) and to find for themselves a framework of meaning in their lives. For RE to be fully balanced it needs to contain these two focuses.

Many RE coordinators have found that colleagues, once their confidence has increased, will very happily teach about the pilgrimage to Makkah, or re-enact in the classroom aspects of the Passover meal. When it comes to the second Attainment Target, however, this new found confidence can suddenly ebb away and there can be a reluctance to roam into the regions of 'meaning'. This will be an area which RE coordinators will have to raise with colleagues both in the early stages of planning RE in the school and later when RE is being monitored, but many will agree with the RE coordinator who wrote:

 *Colleagues were having such difficulty with the second Attainment Target when we were having our early discussions that I judged it best to get them to focus on the first Attainment Target which they were quite happy to do provided that I gave them support and then plan to do further work on the Second Attainment Target later. At least this way, they are all teaching RE to their classes!*

## Balance, continuity and progression

It will be clear from the account of Ninian Smart's work earlier in this chapter that religion is a broad activity and the agreed syllabus map indicates the wide range of areas of which pupils need to have experience. In addition to this it is very important that pupils' understanding should grow and develop and not be a collection of separate and unrelated units. Long-term planning over a key stage or phase needs to ensure that the RE programme is balanced and coherent with continuity and progression. Two issues can illustrate this important question of continuity and progression:

1 in most schools Christmas as a festival features strongly every December. Is there a plan so that pupils' understanding of the festival develops as they move up the school or is each year a repetition of the previous one?
2 if pupils visit, say, a church in Year 3 and a mosque in Year 5 are they just repeating the same activities in each building (e.g. the identification of the key parts) or is their understanding of the significance of a place of worship being developed?

## Which religions to be taught?

Over the years, and before the 1988 Education Reform Act required that the agreed syllabus should reflect the principal religious traditions of Great Britain, aspects of a range of religions, mainly festivals, had been making appearances in many classrooms. Many teachers had concerns that much of this was in danger of giving pupils rather a haphazard experience of religions and could well lead to all sorts of confusion and misunderstanding. The model syllabuses made it quite clear that the legal requirement that agreed syllabuses should reflect the principal religious traditions of the country did not mean necessarily that they should figure in every key stage and the model syllabuses provided a framework within which agreed syllabuses could choose to operate. This framework placed Christianity in each key stage and provided mechanisms for the other traditions to be taught over the four key stages. Because of this a number of more recent agreed syllabuses have made recommendations concerning which religions should be taught, usually Christianity and one other in Key Stage 1 and Christianity and two others in Key Stage 2. There are strong educational arguments for such a focus: it reduces the danger of confusion between religious traditions on the part of pupils, it provides a stronger focus for study, it enables teachers to develop expertise in a more limited area and RE coordinators, in turn, can concentrate their collection of resources similarly.

## Appropriate dimensions

In most Agreed Syllabuses there is an underlying assumption that the areas taught to younger pupils will be marked by a greater concentration on the concrete while the more abstract aspects are more appropriate to the older pupils. This means that in Key Stages 1 and 2 there will be a greater emphasis upon the narrative and mythic dimension (the stories), the practical and ritual dimensions (what people do) and the social and institutional and the material dimensions (buildings, people, places). This does not mean that areas such as doctrines and philosophies will not arise but they are generally more likely to emerge through the other dimensions.

## First hand experience

The most obvious ways of giving pupils first hand experience of a religion is through visits to places of worship or by welcoming a representative of a tradition into school. These are particularly powerful ways of helping religions to come alive in pupils' understanding and imagination. Access to both places of worship and visiting speakers depends to a large extent upon the geographical situation of a school and some are more fortunate in this respect than others. However, all schools must be within a reasonable distance of at least a parish church and these are a very useful resource for many aspects of RE. In planning RE programmes schools need to build in visits and visitors strategically. It is such experiences which not only enliven the subject but also remain in the memory.

## The organisation of teaching

The way in which RE teaching should be organised in a school is an issue which excites considerable discussion. This will vary from school to school according to the ways in which each one plans its curriculum. What matters is that the pupils receive a broad and balanced RE programme.

> What is to be avoided is a former habit in which a teacher would think 'My topic this term is Water. What can I do for RE? Why, Noah's Ark!'

This appending of RE into a topic in this way led to a very fragmented and haphazard experience of RE for pupils. In fact many of them encountered Noah's Ark on a number of occasions as the RE element of topics such as Animals, Weather, Transport and so on! A more appropriate way of linking RE to a topic would be to have a related sub-topic; if for example, the class topic is 'Books', then an appropriate sub-topic might be 'Sacred Books' in which the pupils had the opportunity to look more closely at, say, the Bible and the Qu'ran. This would only be appropriate, though, if it was part of a balanced RE programme for the key stage. Other class topics do not lend themselves so readily to an appropriate RE dimension. In which case it would be more sensible to have an RE mini-topic. Ultimately, though, the principal concern is that pupils should achieve the end of key stage indications of attainment. How this is organised in the school is a secondary matter.

## Conclusion

These are all issues which will need to be considered when a school begins to write its RE policy which will be discussed in the next chapter.

## Chapter 7 Writing a religious education policy

The school policy is a central piece of documentation for RE because it lays out clearly the school's approach to the teaching of the subject. Policies will vary from school to school because they need to fit into and reflect existing school policies on whole school issues such as teaching and learning, assessment, recording, reporting and accountability. Whatever form a policy takes it should reflect the approach to RE in the school, be presented in clear and accessible form to staff members, parents and governors alike and have the broad agreement of both the staff and the governors.

Although there will be local variations, an RE policy would normally include the following sections:
- an introduction which provides a rationale for the subject in the school;
- the legal requirements affecting the provision of RE;
- the aims of RE in the school;
- implementing RE in the school;
- time allocation;
- organisation;
- content;
- cross curricular links;
- equal opportunities;
- special educational needs;
- assessment, recording, reporting and accountability;
- the development of RE.

In developing an RE policy under such headings, the RE coordinator will have to answer a number of key questions after consulting colleagues. What is most important is not who writes the policy but that what is written is known and understood by the staff as a whole and has its broad agreement. If this is not the case, the policy is likely to remain in a pristine state in the filing cabinet!

What follows is an example of an RE policy which follows this pattern:

---

### Hoffham County Primary School

**Religious education policy**
**Introduction**

This policy has been developed by the whole school staff and compiled by a small working group led by the RE coordinator. It also has the approval of the governing body.

The purpose of this document is to provide parents, teachers and governors with a clear summary of the role of RE within the broad education offered by Hoffham Primary School.

We believe that RE has an important part to play in promoting the spiritual, moral, social, cultural and intellectual development of our pupils and in helping them to gain a greater understanding of themselves and a more sympathetic awareness of the needs of others. This enables pupils to be better equipped to cope with the responsibilities and experiences of adult life.

**Legal requirements**

The statutory requirements are to be found in the Education Act (1944) and the Education Reform Act (1988).

1   RE is part of the basic curriculum but not of the National Curriculum. It must be taught according to a locally agreed syllabus prepared by a specially convened standing conference. At Hoffham CP School, RE is taught within the framework of the county agreed syllabus.
2   RE must not be denominational but teaching about denominational differences is permitted.
3   RE must be provided for all registered pupils but parents have the right to withdraw their children from RE lessons.
4   The Educational Reform Act (1988) states that 'RE must reflect the fact that the religious traditions in Great Britain are in the main Christian whilst taking account of the teaching and practices of other principal religions represented in the country'. The county agreed syllabus meets the above requirements.

**The aims of RE in the school**

The school's starting points are the two Attainment Targets in the county agreed syllabus:
1   to develop knowledge and understanding of religion (learning about religion)
2   to explore and respond to human experience (learning from religion)

At Hoffham County Primary School we aim to:
1   help each child develop a sense of his/her own identity and worth and to grow in self-knowledge and confidence;
2   help each child to develop his/her own beliefs so as to acquire a set of moral values which will guide their personal behaviour;

---

3   foster an attitude of fair minded enquiry towards a whole range of religious and non-religious convictions;

4   extend pupils' awareness that people do commit themselves to causes and beliefs;

5   help each pupil to develop the capacity to form individual attitudes and beliefs based on considered opinions even though they may differ from the majority;

6   encourage, respect, understanding and tolerance of those who adhere to different faiths and the ability to recognise prejudice;

7   foster feelings of wonder, delight and mystery and to reflect upon the natural world;

8   help pupils to reflect upon their own patterns of belief and behaviour through exploring religious beliefs and practices with particular reference to Christianity and other major world religions.

## Implementing RE

*Time allocation*

To teach the syllabus effectively it is recognised that children in Key Stage 1 should be allocated one hour per week and in Key Stage 2, one hour and fifteen minutes per week.

*Organisation*

The school curriculum map sets out the organisation of learning opportunities. Subjects are taught in a four year spiral programme over seven years. Care is taken to ensure that pupils have the opportunities to develop their understanding, knowledge, skills and concepts as they move through the school.

A considerable amount of carefully planned RE is implicit and is taught by example and discussions of the pupils' own experiences. Skills such as observing, questioning, discussing, evaluating and reflection are encouraged in all parts of the curriculum but are highlighted in RE. Sensitivity to others and a readiness to listen to others' viewpoints are fostered throughout the curriculum, and especially in RE, Circle Time and PSHE.

More explicit RE is taught in a number of different ways:

1   as an RE element within a class topic;

2   in topics in which RE is the central theme, e.g. Celebrations;

3   (where the class topic does not lend itself easily to RE) as a discrete mini-topic.

*Content*

In Key Stage 1, RE work will focus upon Christianity and Judaism, in Key Stage 2, on Christianity, Islam and Hinduism. This does not mean that there will be no reference to other religions but they will not be the focus.

*Cross curricular links*

Because of the broad nature of RE, it will form natural links with a range of other curriculum areas perhaps notably English, drama, art, history and geography.

*Equal opportunities*

The school believes that it is important for all children to have access to opportunities for spiritual development and awareness and for understanding of the great religious traditions.

*Special educational needs*

RE is taught at a level appropriate to the age, ability and experience of the pupils and is therefore accessible to all.

## Assessment, recording, reporting and accountability

The county agreed syllabus lays down end of key stage targets and these are built into our scheme of work. Evidence is gathered mainly through observation, oral discussion, written tasks and drawing. The recorded evidence assists teachers both in their planning and in their reporting to parents and governors.

Examples of work, including photographs, will be kept in a school portfolio for future comparisons.

The development of RE

1  The scheme of work in RE will be developed continuously during its introduction.
2  Teaching and learning in relation to the policy and scheme of work will be monitored by the headteacher and RE coordinator.
3  Necessary resources will be identified and financial provision made for them annually.
4  Inservice training will be provided for the RE coordinator and other members of staff as necessary.
5  RE will be a focus for review and development in accordance with the agreed three year cycle of curriculum development.

*Part four*

# Developing religious education in the school

**Chapter 8**
Planning the religious education curriculum

**Chapter 9**
Monitoring and evaluating religious education

**Chapter 10**
Assessment, recording, reporting and accountability

## Chapter 8    Planning the religious education curriculum

## Long-, medium- and short-term planning — in outline

Effective planning is the major factor in ensuring that the experience which pupils receive is of good quality. Of course, for good quality RE there also needs to be willing informed teachers, but without an overall plan, even the most willing teaching is likely to be haphazard and spasmodic. Planning is normally done in three stages: long-term, medium-term and short-term.

### Long-term planning

A long-term plan is effectively a broad outline of what will be taught and when during each year group over a whole school. Its purpose is:

■ to provide for coverage of the local Agreed Syllabus;
■ to ensure balance and progression across the key stages each year and to avoid repetition;
■ to define broadly a pupil's entitlement to RE across the appropriate key stage;
■ to make appropriate links with other subject areas;
■ to outline the year's work for each teacher.

### Medium-term planning

Medium-term planning (sometimes called the Scheme of Work) is concerned with taking the units within the long-term plan and developing them. An effective plan for the development of one of these units would normally include:

- identifying learning intentions;
- providing an outline of content;
- identifying teaching strategies and learning activities;
- identifying focuses for assessments;
- identifying resources;
- identifying curriculum links (where appropriate).

### Short-term planning

Short-term planning is normally undertaken by the classteacher (occasionally with support from the RE coordinator). This is the normal lesson planning that any teacher is used to in this phase. This includes:

- identifying clear learning outcomes;
- making provision for differing abilities in the class;
- identifying assessment opportunities;
- planning the pattern of the lesson;
- identifying any special groupings of pupils;
- identification of resources.

## Long-term planning

Long-term planning will reflect both the Programmes of Study and the end of key stage indications of attainment in the local Agreed Syllabus and the school's RE policy. Together these provide the framework of the long-term plan. Often an RE coordinator will undertake an audit prior to the devising of the long-term plan to see what is in place already. Long-term plans will differ from school to school in a local education authority because, although the Agreed Syllabus will be common to all, the RE policies of the individual schools will vary to some degree as they will reflect different compositions of school staffs and also different school planning frameworks.

In attempting in this chapter to move beyond the principles of long-term planning, it is harder in RE than in National

Curriculum subjects simply because there is no nationally prescribed syllabus for RE and agreed syllabuses, although generally moving in a similar direction, are not identical. The plan therefore is to take an RE coordinator's account of the long-term plan for her school, one which would fit fairly well with many agreed syllabuses. It is not presented as perfect — in fact, it has a number of weaknesses of which different readers will be aware — but, on balance, it is a very useful basis for planning RE in the school.

---

We based our long-term plan on our local Agreed Syllabus and our RE policy, which took some time to hammer out. In the end I was pleased with the result; it was not exactly what I would have decided but it was near enough to that and it did reflect the views and interests of the staff, and it is a stable staff.

The principles which lay behind our long term plan were:
- The two religions to be focused upon in Key Stage 1 are Christianity and Judaism and the three in Key Stage 2 are Christianity, Hinduism and Islam.
- While we intend to focus on these very strongly, we are not prevented from making reference to aspects of other religions.
- On the whole the staff is concerned about causing confusion in children's minds, what one called mishmash, so on the whole we prefer RE work to focus on one religion at a time rather than have a thematic approach (although there are some themes in the plan).
- As a continuation of this, we decided in Key Stage 2 to have Christianity in each year group but to block the other two religions namely Hinduism in Years 4 and 6 and Islam in Years 3 and 5.
- We recognise the importance of providing pupils with the opportunities to enrich their experience so that religious ideas and concepts will have a richer meaning. There is therefore a balance between our two Attainment Targets.
- We tried to plan for progression and this is perhaps most noticeable in the provision for the annual celebration of both Christmas and Easter which we wanted to be both progressive and varied.

Here follows our long-term plan. It is broken down into years and terms and identifies topics with related ideas and resources.

---

## Medium-term planning

Once the long-term planning is in place, it becomes necessary to take the individual units in order to give them more substance. This may be done by the class teacher but it may well be that the coordinator has to work with class teachers to develop the individual units appropriately. Together all the units so developed will make up the RE scheme of work.

There are no rules as to how a scheme of work/medium-term planning has to look, and this will vary from school to school,

**Long-term plan for RE**

**Reception**

| | Topics | Ideas, resources |
|---|---|---|
| A U T U M N | Celebration<br><br>Harvest festival | Share in a form of celebration<br>Talk about birthdays<br>Share in a harvest celebration<br>Help distribute goods<br>Talk about the beauties of nature and of the seasons |
| C H R I S T M A S | A baby is born | Discuss preparations for the birth of a baby<br>Talk about Mary's long journey and the birth in the stable |
| S P R I N G | Ourselves | Discuss how everyone is special and important<br>Bring in things which are special to them, e.g. toys, books<br>Discuss why these things are special<br>Special people who care for them at home and at school<br>Discuss why these people are special |
| E A S T E R | Easter: new life | Brief account of the death and resurrection of Jesus<br>Focus on new life and hope: spring time, symbolism of Easter eggs |
| S U M M E R | Our world | Explore and respond to the wonders of nature<br>Use seasons to explore changes in the natural world<br>Grow seeds<br>How to live in our world<br>Why do we need rules?<br>What sort of rules do we need? |

## Year 1

| | Topics | Ideas, resources |
|---|---|---|
| A U T U M N | Caring and helping | 'The Good Shepherd'<br>Care of all living creatures<br>Attitude to each other<br>Attitude towards animals<br>Work of RSPCA |
| | Well known stories | Enjoy hearing stories, e.g. Samson, King David, Joseph |
| C H R I S T M A S | Jesus, a very special baby | Retell the birth story<br>Introduce the story of Gabriel's message to Mary and the visit of the shepherds |
| S P R I N G | Festivals (Judaism) | Hear stories behind the festival of Hanukkah |
| E A S T E R | Jesus: a loving person | Accounts of the Last Supper, the Betrayal by Judas, the crucifixion and resurrection with a focus on the love within the cruel events |
| S U M M E R | Friendships | Discussion of what makes a good/bad friend<br>Identification of key qualities which make up friendship — help, trust etc. Examples of people who have been good friends to others, e.g. Mother Teresa of Calcutta |

**Year 2**

| | Topics | Ideas, resources |
|---|---|---|
| A U T U M N | Beginning and growing | Birth — baby photographs |
| | | Baptism — enact one |
| | | Visit a church |
| | | Barmitzvah / Batmitzvah |
| | Living together | Discuss friendship and quarrels |
| | | Making up |
| | | Jesus' teaching on love and forgiveness |
| | | Stories of Good Samaritan and the Prodigal/Lost Son |
| C H R I S T M A S | Jesus: love and hate | Retell the birth stories |
| | | Introduce the role of Herod and the family's |
| | | flight into Egypt |
| | | Visit of the Magi |
| S P R I N G | The Bible | Special book for Christians |
| | | Opportunity to see various versions |
| | Jewish festivals | The Sabbath — how it is kept |
| | | Its significance for Jews and for Judaism |
| | | Sabbath artefacts |
| | | Passover — the stories associated with the Passover seder |
| | | Passover artefacts |
| E A S T E R | Lent and Easter | Shrove Tuesday, Ash Wednesday, Mothering Sunday |
| | | Palm Sunday story with Palm Cross |
| S U M M E R | Judaism | Importance of the Torah |
| | | Torah Scroll |
| | | Visit synagogue |
| | | Introduction to 10 Commandments |
| | | Mezuzah, Tefillin |
| | | Tallith |
| | | Importance of the Torah for Jews |

**Year 3**

|   | Topics | Ideas, resources |
|---|---|---|
| A | Myself — My family | Belonging, Self-worth |
| U | My home | Living in community |
| T | Friendship (Sharing) | Jesus' friends, disciples |
| U | The story of Mohammed | Key facts of his life; Five pillars of Islam |
| M | Precious things | Personal special things |
| N | Exploring artefacts | A look at a few key artefacts |
| C | Advent | Retell both stories |
| H |  | Focus on waiting and expectation |
| R |  | Advent Corona and Advent Calendar |
| I |  | Story of Simeon in the Temple |
| S |  |  |
| T |  |  |
| M |  |  |
| A |  |  |
| S |  |  |
| S | Rites of passage in | Baptism — what happens? |
| P | Christianity | Symbolism of water and candles/Paschal candle |
| R |  | Marriage — what happens? |
| I |  | Symbolism of vows and the rings |
| N |  | Death — funeral services |
| G |  |  |
| E | Easter: the first | Focus on the reactions of the disciples to the Easter |
| A | witnesses | events: Peter, Mary Magdalene |
| S |  | The part played by Pontius Pilate |
| T |  |  |
| E |  |  |
| R |  |  |
| S | Symbols | Consider the function of symbols |
| U |  | Identify, e.g. the fish (icthus) the Crescent, the AUM |
| M |  | Special clothing, e.g. ihran at the hajj |
| M |  | Special food, e.g. hot cross buns |
| E |  | Special features, e.g. water at Baptism |
| R | Visit to mosque | Place of prayer in Islam — prayer mats and compass |
|  |  | Identify the component parts of a Mosque |
|  |  | (internal and external) |
|  |  | Discuss their meaning and purpose |
|  |  | Significance of wudu |

## Year 4

|  | Topics | Ideas, resources |
|---|---|---|
| **A U T U M N** | Who is Jesus?<br><br><br>Christian worship | A preacher, healer, teacher<br>Examples of these roles from Gospels<br>Son of God?<br>Well known prayers (e.g. Lord's Prayer)<br>Holy Communion — bread and wine<br>Hymns and music<br>Changing moods — thanksgiving at Harvest, joy at<br>Christmas, sadness on Good Friday |
| **C H R I S T M A S** | Christmas around<br>the world | Christingles<br>Stories of Baboushka, St. Lucy and St. Nicolas |
| **S P R I N G** | Worship in Hinduism | Forms of Hindu worship<br>Individual devotion to your own murti<br>Puja corner in home<br>Puja tray<br>Visit to Hindu Temple<br>Prashad<br>Arti |
| **E A S T E R** | Symbols of Easter | Empty cross, the empty tomb<br>The Paschal Candle, the New Fire |
| **S U M M E R** | Rites of passage<br>in Hinduism<br><br><br><br><br>Hindu settlement<br>in Britain | Reference to<br>   Birth and naming ceremonies<br>   The sacred thread ceremony<br>   Marriage<br>   Death<br>The role of the householder the monk and the sanyasi<br>Patterns of settlement<br>The role of the temple/mandir |

**Year 5**

|  | Topics | Ideas, resources |
|---|---|---|
| A<br>U<br>T<br>U<br>M<br>N | Festivals and<br>pilgrimage in Islam<br><br>Pilgrimage in<br>Christianity | The Haij and Id-ul-Adha<br>Ramadan and Id-ul-Fitr<br>What happens and why<br>The idea of the special/sacred place<br>The purpose of pilgrimages<br>Jerusalem and the Via Dolorosa<br>Lourdes — healing<br>Walsingham |
| C<br>H<br>R<br>I<br>S<br>T<br>M<br>A<br>S | Christmas through art | Collect representations of the Nativity — postcards, slides,<br>Christmas cards<br>Pupils to analyse themes and messages within them |
| S<br>P<br>R<br>I<br>N<br>G | Creation stories<br><br><br><br>Some issues in<br>Muslim family life | Examples of Creation stories in Christianity, Islam and<br>Hinduism<br>Distinguish between literal accounts and symbolic accounts<br>What do the Creation stories say about the world?<br>Close relationships in the extended family. Arranged<br>marriages<br>Second and third generation Muslims in Britain |
| E<br>A<br>S<br>T<br>E<br>R | Easter through art | Collect slides and postcards of crucifixion and<br>resurrection of Jesus<br>Use analyses of these as a basis for discussion<br>on the meaning of the events |
| S<br>U<br>M<br>M<br>E<br>R | Who is my<br>neighbour?<br><br><br>Jesus — teaching | Issues of interdependence and brotherhood. Zakah and<br>Khums in Islam<br>Work of Christian Aid, CAFOD and/or TEAR Fund,<br>Red Cross and Red Crescent<br>Concern for the outcast: stories of Lost Sheep,<br>Prodigal Son, Zaccheus<br>The Good Samaritan |

**Year 6**

| | Topics | Ideas, resources |
|---|---|---|
| A U T U M N | How the Bible came to us | Early manuscripts/codices<br>Illuminated manuscripts — Lindisfarne Gospels<br>Printing — William Caxton<br>Authorised Version 1611<br>Recent translations |
| | Divali | Underlying story and practices<br>Detailed considerations of the story of Rama and Sita looking at its meaning for Hindus. |
| C H R I S T M A S | Christmas:<br>the two accounts | Read the birth stories in Matthew and Luke<br>Discuss and identify their similarities and differences<br>What is each saying about Jesus? |
| S P R I N G | Some Hindu beliefs | One God yet many images<br>Ideas of Karma and Moksha<br>Artefacts — images of chief 'gods' |
| | Death and beyond | Views of Christianity, Islam<br>Hinduism and Judaism on death and what follows it<br>Coping with grief |
| E A S T E R | Easter:<br>the gospel accounts | Read the accounts of the trial, of death and resurrection of Jesus in two gospels<br>Discuss and identify similarities and differences<br>What is each saying about Jesus |
| S U M M E R | The church and the community | Visit church<br>Identify various services<br>Check church newsletter and noticeboard<br>Interview priest/minister about the broader work of church and in wider community |
| | Faith and commitment | Faith into action<br>Biographies drawn from 2 of St. Francis of Assisi<br>Father Damien<br>William Wilberforce<br>Martin Luther King<br>Helder Camara |

but it should give an indication of learning intentions, outline of content, some intimation of teaching strategies and activities and some opportunities for assessment.

Below is an example of how one of the units, Pilgrimage in Christianity, proposed in Year 5 of the long-term plan was developed.

---

**Development of the unit:**

**Pilgrimage in Christianity**
Year 5
Number of hours: 8

*Learning intentions*
- begin to understand the notion of a sacred place
- know the customs involved in making a pilgrimage
- develop an understanding of how pilgrimage can deepen spirituality and heighten awareness of community involvement

*Outline of content*
- discussion of why some places are special/sacred in Christianity
- look at case studies drawn from Jerusalem (especially the Via Dolorosa), Lourdes and Walsingham
- what is involved in making a pilgrimage, extracts from *Canterbury Tales*
- discussion of pilgrimage as symbol of the journey of the human soul to God
- talk by a pilgrim to Lourdes

*Teaching strategies and activities*
- discussion
- video of pilgrimage
- visiting speaker
- produce booklet
- imaginative writing on being a pilgrim

*Assessment*
All pupils are expected to produce a booklet which will enable them to 'describe the customs and feelings involved in making a pilgrimage' (end of key stage indicator of attainment).

---

## Short-term planning

The above unit on 'Pilgrimage in Christianity' will, before it is presented to pupils, have to be organised and arranged into a series of lessons, each one of which will need to meet the criteria as laid out earlier in this chapter. Normally short term planning would be the responsibility of the class teacher though RE coordinators are often involved when the subject matter is felt to be particularly difficult.

## Chapter 9　Monitoring and evaluating religious education

An important aspect of the coordinator's role is the monitoring of the subject throughout the school and making some evaluation of pupils' progress. The essential rationale for monitoring is that subject coordinators have responsibility for ensuring that their subject is delivered as planned in the school and, if it is not, to identify the reasons and to find ways in which any difficulties can be overcome. In practice this is happening to some extent informally but a more formal approach does enable judgments about the quality of children's learning to be made more effectively. Although monitoring and evaluation is clearly an essential part of managing teaching and learning — what is the point of devising policy and plans if no one looks to see how well they have been implemented? — many coordinators shy away from their monitoring role mainly because they fear to be seen as a spy in colleagues' classrooms! This needs to be discounted as the process of monitoring and evaluation within a school should be a means of identifying needs and providing support where required. Often it is the method of monitoring rather than the motive for doing it which causes the concern!

In some senses it can be harder to make judgments about pupils making progress in a subject such as RE than in, say, practical subjects but there are measures which can be used and coordinators should bear them in mind when monitoring RE in their school.

These measures include:

- a broadening and more extensive knowledge of the faith and practice of religions and a growing awareness of the relationship between the two;
- the capacity of pupils to handle increasingly complex concepts and ideas;
- the ability to revise earlier judgments when confronted with new material;
- a developing capacity in pupils to test religious statements against their own experience.

There will be different focuses in monitoring and evaluating RE and these can be planned over a number of years. Realistically, given the busy world of the primary school, it is unlikely that there will be very much opportunity to undertake any extensive activity. It will therefore be the responsibility of the school's senior management team along with the RE coordinator to identify a highly focused monitoring activity preferably obtruding as little as possible into teaching time.

This issue of *finding the time* to undertake the monitoring and evaluation of RE (and other subjects too) will always be a difficulty especially with the ever increasing focus upon English and mathematics in the curriculum. This makes it specially important to focus on the minimum number of aspects felt necessary to undertake the task. The situation can be eased in a number of ways, for example:

- using non contact time effectively;
- discussions at staff meetings and staff training days;
- discussions with colleagues on an individual basis at break and lunch time;
- overseeing colleagues' short term planning in RE;
- sampling children's work;
- involving others such as the member of the governing body with oversight for RE;
- combining the activity with the classroom-based support of another teacher.

## Possible strategies

Possible strategies for monitoring and evaluating RE in school include the following:

- examining pupils' work in RE;
- observing and listening to pupils and teachers at work during RE sessions;
- talking to pupils about their work;
- discussing with teachers.

| Some examples of possible strategies | |
|---|---|
| Activity | Monitoring/evaluation strategies |
| 1  Pupils' standards in RE | i   Review the work of a selected sample of pupils. How does it match with the expectations of the agreed syllabus?<br>ii  Monitor teachers' marking.<br>iii Observe pupils being taught and identify strengths and weaknesses in their knowledge and understanding. |
| 2  Pupils' progress through the school | Compare a sample of work from different age groups. Look for progress and development in terms of the demands of the task, breadth of material studied, capacity of pupils to make comparisons. |
| 3  Range and quality of pupils' work | i   Check the schemes of work to ensure that they match up to the requirements of the Agreed Syllabus.<br>ii  Identify specified opportunities for focus upon the pupils' own spiritual education. |
| 4  Teachers' expertise and confidence | i   Identify with teachers their individual strengths and weaknesses.<br>ii  Attempt to provide opportunities for team teaching to build confidence. |

## Focuses for monitoring

Bearing in mind the pressure for time in the primary curriculum, monitoring of all subjects, including RE, which are not core subjects, must realistically be focused sharply over a narrow aspect which will change every year. Below are four possible focuses with an indication of the sorts of questions which might be asked:

### 1  Looking at the quality of pupils' learning and progress

The following questions might prove useful:
- do pupils use similar skills of enquiry in a range of contexts?
- are pupils able to write/talk about the traditions they have been taught?
- how aware are the pupils of religious issues?

This focus can be monitored by observations of teaching, by talking to pupils and to teachers and examining a sample of pupil work.

- are pupils able to apply religious traditions to everyday life?
- are pupils able to use correct terminology when describing, say, religious traditions in the area?
- are pupils encouraged to learn *from* religions as well as learning *about* religions? Is there a balance?
- do pupils have the opportunity to engage in reasoned discussion and debate in the classroom?
- are opportunities provided through books, videos, ICT and CD–ROM for some degree of independent study?
- do pupils achieve the end of key stage indications of attainment?

## 2 Looking at the effectiveness of teaching RE

When observing the teaching of RE the following questions might prove useful as a means both of measuring success in the teaching of the subject and also of leading to further evaluation with individual teachers:

- are the pupils motivated by the work undertaken?
- are the learning intentions clear and achievable?
- is the teaching well paced?
- is the work well matched to pupil age and ability?
- are appropriate and varied strategies being used?
- are there opportunities for discussion?
- is teacher intervention appropriate and effective?
- are the tasks set sufficiently demanding?
- what is the quality of feedback to pupils?
- what provision is made for pupils with special needs to gain access to the RE teaching?

This focus can be monitored largely by observing RE lessons supplemented by discussion with pupils and teachers and some sampling of pupils's work.

## 3 Assessment, recording and reporting

The following questions might prove useful:

- are assessment arrangements manageable and do they meet the requirements of the Agreed Syllabus?
- is assessment used formatively so that pupils know how to improve their work?
- is assessment used to inform future planning?
- is assessment seen as a helpful, positive process?
- is reporting to parents/carers effective?

This can be undertaken largely through observation and inspection of the appropriate documentation.

This focus can be undertaken largely by examining the range of resources against the RE policy and planning and through a small amount of observation and discussion with teachers.

## 4 Resources for RE

The following questions might prove useful:
■ are the resources adequate to support the teaching of RE?
■ are the religions focused on the religions taught?
■ are the resources broadly based including books, videos, artefacts and CD-ROM?
■ do pupils have easy access to resources?
■ are the teachers aware of the significance of the artefacts used?

There is always a danger that monitoring and evaluation is done because it always is done, a report is made and things go on as they did before. Undertaken properly, monitoring and evaluation is concerned with such issues as entitlement, quality and improvement. All teaching can be improved and out of the annual monitoring and evaluation exercise should emerge strategies for development to enhance the RE experience of pupils during the following year.

## Chapter 10

# Assessment, recording, reporting and accountability

The process of assessment, recording and reporting has become an increasingly important area of development in schools since the Education Reform Act of 1988. This does not mean that teachers before this date did not assess the work their pupils were doing nor keep records nor report back to parents either orally at a parents' consultation evening or through the written school report. Since 1988 however there has been a statutory requirement that in the core subjects assessments will be made (and published) at 7, 11 and 14 and 16 and that each child's progress in all the foundation subjects must be reported annually to parents.

There is no national statutory requirement for the assessment of pupils in RE except that RE is subject to the local Agreed Syllabus and most, if not all, of these require that pupils' progress in RE should be assessed and that this should be reported to parents/carers.

## The purpose of assessment

In broad terms, assessment is usually perceived to have four main interlocking purposes:

1   *informative* — assessment finds out what progress has been made and this information can be conveyed to pupils and their parents;

2 *formative* — in this way pupils can be helped to be involved in the assessment process;

3 *diagnostic* — assessing pupils' progress identifies strengths and weaknesses and enables teachers to act accordingly;

4 *summative* — assessment makes it possible to present a record of attainment at a particular stage.

In practical terms, for most teachers, assessing RE enables them to *measure* the progress of pupils in the subject. This in turn enables them to know with some precision the level of attainment of individual pupils so that they can provide additional support for those who require it. Similarly pupils themselves can become more clearly aware of areas which for them need development. Only with this knowledge are teachers able to report securely to parents on the progress of their children; general impression unsupported by any firm evidence is a poor basis for such reporting. Assessment too is part of the monitoring and evaluation process. There is an educational jingle which goes 'plan, do, review' and assessment provides teachers with an opportunity to evaluate their own effectiveness in planning and doing and can therefore lead to a review both of the teaching content and delivery.

## Assessing in RE

Talk of assessing RE can cause an instant concern in some teachers because of fear that such an assessment will intrude upon a pupil's proper privacy. It is therefore important as RE coordinator to ensure that teachers in your school are quite clear about what is and what is not being assessed. There should be no intention of assessing pupils' orthodoxy or whether they have or do not have a religious commitment, or whether they have 'right' or 'wrong' values. These would be quite inappropriate areas to assess given the aims and intended outcomes of RE in schools. Rather it is pupils' knowledge and understanding which is the subject of assessment. Pupils are taught, for example, a considerable amount of information about religions and part of the assessment will be the ability to recall significant facts, to see them within a context and to communicate them clearly either in speech or writing. Beyond this pupils are helped to see the implications of religious belief upon ways of living and for moral issues. These, for example, would be entirely appropriate areas to assess and would not intrude in any way into a pupil's privacy.

## Criteria for effective assessment

- assessment is an essential part of the learning process and not something bolted on;
- assessment tasks are related to the learning intentions;
- teachers' judgments are based on an informed knowledge and understanding of religions;
- planned assessment tasks are realistic both in the demands of the activity and the frequency of that implementation.

It is important to emphasise two of these points. Firstly, all teachers when delivering RE should have identified clear learning intentions in their planning. Assessment should seek to discover to what extent these have been achieved. On a larger scale too most Agreed Syllabuses identify end of key stage indicators of attainment. Assessment at the end of a key stage will be related to these statements. Secondly, assessment must be manageable otherwise it will not be successful. If, for example, there are three RE topics a year, one assessment task for each is likely to be both achievable and adequate.

In this way, evidence starts to accumulate from formative assessment which is an integral part of teaching and the means whereby teachers begin to build up a picture of their pupils' needs, achievements and abilities. This leads on in turn to summative assessment which is reached by using the information gleaned from formative assessment to form a judgment about pupils' overall levels of achievement. Identifying summative achievement may also be supplemented by specific assessment tasks related to end of key stage indicators of attainment as described in the example below.

This is an account by an RE coordinator of approaches in his junior school to the summative assessing of RE:

Assessment in RE has caused some ruffled fathers among one or two colleagues because, basically, they are still working their way into a non-confessional approach to RE. However, we did agree in Year 6 that we would undertake a formal assessment on the children's understanding of festivals. Some colleagues thought the best approach to it would be through observation and discussion but I felt that we needed to collect some hard evidence which I could keep in preparation for any inspection which might come our way.

Our agreed syllabus expects that at the end of Key Stage 2 pupils should be able to show an understanding and knowledge of religious festivals and ceremonies and this understanding and knowledge should involve both being able to describe how two different festivals or ceremonies are celebrated and give reasons why they are celebrated.

The children had studied examples of both festivals and what we call 'rites of passage' so they had covered major festivals such as Christmas, Easter, Passover, Divali and Id-ul-Fitr and also, as examples of rites of passage, baptism, weddings, bar-mitzvahs and the sacred thread ceremony.

We therefore set the pupils a task which was designed to elicit their general knowledge of the structure of an identified festival or ceremony and their awareness of the reasons behind the festival. We 'brainstormed' for a few minutes about the assessment task: write a guide for tourists about a festival to be held, produce a booklet on baptism for parents, produce a tape explaining the significance of a festival, give a group presentation on. . . . In the end we opted to offer a choice, either the guide for tourists or the book for parents.

The actual tasks were enjoyed by the pupils who showed that in general they had met this end of key stage indicator of attainment and I also had my evidence!

Although this task had been used to assess an end of key stage indicator of attainment, it could equally be used as a piece of formative assessment in an RE topic in Key Stage 2. In many ways it is important to spread assessment of end of key stage indicators of attainment more widely over the year groups otherwise Year 2 and Year 6 might become impossible to manage.

## Differing levels of response

In any assessment exercise there will be considerable variation in the quality of the response. Here another RE coordinator muses upon an early foray into assessment:

My own class is Year 5 and we had been doing a unit on prayer and worship in Islam. My learning intentions were that the children should learn about prayer and worship in Islam because of its centrality in that religion and through this study enrich their own understanding of the nature of prayer in general. The content planned was:

Pupils should be able to:

**The mosque**
- name some essential feature of a mosque and show some understanding of their function;
- understand the role of the mosque for Muslims;

■ understand the importance of symbols and rituals in the mosque;
■ know about the role of the Imam.

**Worship**
■ understand the importance of prayer and of its frequency for Muslims;
■ recognise that worship is a response to Allah.

I intended to assess over the whole topic through discussion and observation but I also identified a specific assessment opportunity. Here I wanted the children to demonstrate that they had some *understanding* of worship in Islam so I set them the task: 'You have a Muslim friend. Persuade him/her to write you a letter explaining why prayer is so important to Muslims'.

The response to this task was both very interesting and very useful. It ranged from basically — 'we are brought up to it so we have to do it' to the notion that 'Muslims believe that God is the creator and sustainer of all things and that his very being demands our worship. Worship five times is a refreshment and a joy because we lose ourselves in his greatness'. The range therefore was from a level of no understanding to a very sophisticated perception. Most pupils came between! It did raise the question for me as to what does meeting the learning intentions actually mean. Clearly the first pupil quoted appeared to have no understanding at all, though he did know about the five prayer times each day. The pupil at the other extreme met the learning intentions superbly. I don't really think that I have time to work out detailed levels of understanding. I think that I shall just have to record those who didn't appear to understand as having failed to meet the learning intentions and do some remedial work with them and to reward the rest as having met it to some degree with perhaps an asterisk for those who show special perception!

## Recording

Recording is a highly important activity in the assessment process because teachers' memories are fallible. First and foremost recording acts as an *aide memoire* for teachers. Because it is recording the results of assessments made, whether ongoing or at the end of the key stage, it should act as a powerful and tangible source of information for future planning in the subject, for future teachers who will want to build on firm evidence and for reporting to parents on the achievement of their children. Recording should focus upon what pupils can do and so it can be a celebration of achievement though at the same time noting areas which should be developed.

There are different types of recording. There is the more informal approach which operates on a day to day basis and the more formal approach using systems which operate across a whole school. Whatever system is in use it must be simple, manageable and easy to handle. If it is not it will cease to be used sufficiently because it will prove too time consuming. If it does not provide the evidence too to help teachers to plan the next stage of learning nor the evidence of reporting to parents then it will be seen as an expensive luxury and cease to be undertaken other than in a perfunctory way.

There is a variety of ways of recording achievement which are worth considering:

■ *A school portfolio*
This would be a portfolio of work in RE undertaken over a period of time. This can be very useful in that it can both provide a visual standard of reasonably achievable work which can be very helpful for teachers less confident in the subject and also for parents and governors.

■ *Individual portfolio*
A number of teachers find it very useful to keep a small collection of the work of individual pupils suitably annotated. This can be a very useful source of evidence in discussions with parents and in the task of drawing up a profile at the end of a key stage.

■ *A record book*
Many teachers keep an ongoing record book, a page for each child upon which they note down significant information about the pupil. Significant observation about RE should also be recorded in this book.

■ *An individual pupil record sheet*
It is possible to devise a record sheet for RE which can be carried forward by the pupil over a school career. To create one of these it is important to identify what information needs to be recorded, for example, understanding the Programmes of Study, pupils' attitude and commitment to the work.

■ *Pupil self-assessments*
Pupils can be encouraged to be involved in assessment of their own work and performance. This involves teachers discussing progress with pupils, explaining the learning outcomes of the work and the approaches to assessment. In this way pupils can begin to identify their strengths and those areas upon which they will need to develop. Older pupils can keep an ongoing record of their progress.

Many schools will have whole school assessment and recording approaches such as records of achievement into which RE will fit. Some of the above approaches however do produce the sort of firm evidence which is needed for *reporting*.

### Reporting RE

Reporting to parents should be based firmly upon the evidence of a pupil's performance based upon assessment activities which have been recorded accurately. The statement should, therefore, be an accurate reflection of the pupil's performance based upon the teacher's assessment. It should explain clearly the pupil's achievement across the range of Programmes of Study and should also focus upon the positive achievements of the pupil along with areas for improvement. The report will therefore be summative and individual achievement will be placed in the context of what the pupils have undertaken in RE and what the school is trying to achieve.

## Accountability

It should be clear from this account that assessment, recording and reporting — and to some extent also monitoring which has been considered in a previous chapter — are all intimately related to each other and jointly they represent the school's accountability to parents and the wider community. Schools plan learning experiences for pupils based on learning intentions which they develop from syllabuses, whether National Curriculum or, in the case of RE, local Agreed Syllabuses, provided by the wider community. These learning experiences are then carefully assessed and these assessments recorded so that schools can know much more accurately how groups and individuals have benefited from the teaching. This in turn, enables schools to assess the needs of individuals and of whole classes and to respond to these in subsequent planning. This collection of evidence and the formal reporting of it to parents either orally or in writing is highly symbolic of the accountability of schools to those who maintain them.

*Part five*   Useful resources

**Chapter 11**
Books, artefacts, videos and ICT

**Chapter 12**
Visits and visitors

**Chapter 13**
Some useful addresses

## Chapter 11    Books, artefacts, videos and ICT

## Books for teachers

### Teaching RE

*Religious Education 5–12*, D. Bastide: Falmer Press, 1987.

*Good Practice in Primary RE*, D. Bastide: Falmer Press, 1992.

*New Methods in RE Teaching: An Experiential Approach*, John Hammond et al.: Oliver and Boyd, 1990.

*How Do I Teach RE?*, Westhill Project manual by G. Read, J. Rudge, G. Teece and R. Howarth: Stanley Thornes, 1992 (2nd. ed.)

*Religious Education in the Primary Curriculum*, W. Owen Cole and Judith Evans-Lowndes: RMEP, 1991.

*Religious Education Across the Curriculum*, J. Rankin, A. Brown and M. Hayward: Longman, 1991.

*Religious Education Topics for the Primary School*, J. Rankin, A. Brow and M. Hayward: Longman, 1989.

*A Gift to the Child: Religious Education in the Primary School*, (Teachers' Source Book) M. Grimmitt, J. Grove and L. Spencer: Simon and Schuster, 1991.

*First Topics Series*, (Autumn, Spring, Summer) D. J. Taylor (Notes for teachers on laying RE foundations in KS1) and *Open the Door* (introducing Christianity): BFSS National RE Centre.

*Handbook for Religious Education*, (KS1 and 2) Solihull Metropolitan Borough.

*The Junior RE Handbook* (Ed.) R. Jackson and D. Starkings: Stanley Thornes, 1990.

## World religions

*Teaching World Religions* (A Teacher's Handbook), C. Erricker (Ed.): Heinemann, 1993.

*Six Religions in the 20th Century*, W. Owen Cole with Peggy Morgan: Hulton Educational, 1984.

*World Religions Series*, (6 books), W. Owen Cole (Ed.): Stanley Thornes, 1989.

*World Religions in Education*, SHAP Working Party 1988.

*Faith and Commitment Series*, Sylvia and Barrie Sutcliffe: RMEP, 1994.

*Belief and Practice Series*, (Ed.) Jan Thompson: Hodder and Stoughton, 1984.

*Multi-faith Topics in the Primary School* (Christianity, Hinduism, Islam, Judaism), J. Webb: Cassell, 1990.

Living Religions: Teachers' Handbook, C. Richards (Ed.): Nelson, 1998.

## Festivals

*Festivals Together*, Sue Fizjohn, Minda Weston, Judy Large: Hawthorn Press, 1993.

*Festivals*, compiled by Jill Bennett: Scholastic Publications, 1994.

*Festival!* (Ramadan and Eid-ul-Fitr, Carnival, Diwali, Chinese New Year), Macmillan Education, 1986 (Teachers' notes and pupils' worksheets).

*Living Festivals*, (series editor) Jack Priestley: RMEP, 1983. (Hannukah, Chinese New Year, Christmas, Divali, Easter, Festivals of the Buddha, Guru Nanak's Birthday, Hallowe'en/All Souls'/All Saints', Holi, Holy Week, Passover, Ramadan and Id-ul-Fitr, Shabbat, Shrove Tuesday/Ash Wednesday) Also *Jewish Festivals Omnibus*, 1993, and *Christian Festivals Omnibus*, 1994, and *Teachers' Books* on Jewish, Christian, Muslim and Hindu festivals with photocopiable material.

*Celebrations: Festivals in a Multi-faith Community*, Celia Collinson and Campbell Miller: Hodder and Stoughton, 1990. (Hindu, Jewish, Christian, Muslim, Sikh).

*Teaching RE: Festivals 5–11*, CEM.

*SHAP Calendar of Religious Festivals*, SHAP Working Party. (Annual)

*Harvest Festival in World Religions*, E. Brown: BFSS National RE Centre.

## General themes

*Exploring Religion Series*: Bell and Hyman. (People, Buildings, Worship, Writings, Festivals, Signs and Symbols)

*Pilgrimages: Journeys from a Multi-faith Community*: Hodder and Stoughton, 1990.

*Exploring a Theme*: CEM (Myself, Seasons, Places of Worship, Journeys, Food, Communities, Fire, Water, Signs and Symbols, Barriers, Time, Leaders).

*Teaching RE*, CEM booklets on *Symbol 5–11, Worship 5–11, Harvest 5–14*.

*Folens Primary RE Series* (Key Figures, Special Times, Expressing Belief, People and Worship, Creation) 1993.

*Life Themes in the Early Years*, (Pack 1: The Natural World, Celebration. Pack 2: Stages of Life, Lifestyles. Pack 3: Relationships and Rules, Issues) Westhill: Stanley Thornes, 1990.

*Bridges to Religions*, (The Warwick RE Project) Materials for KS1: Heinemann, 1995. (5 pupil books and teacher resource book)

## Using artefacts

*Religious Artefacts in the Classroom*, Paul Gateshill and Jan Thompson, Hodder and Stoughton, 1995.

*Islamic, Hindu, Jewish, Christian and Sikh Artefacts*, (5 booklets), published by SECRU, Shropshire Education Curriculum Resources Unit, 1992.

*Using Artefacts in Religious Education: Classroom Strategies for Primary Teachers*, Christine Howard: RMEP, 1995.

## Relating to specific religions

### Buddhism

*The Wisdom of the Buddha*, Jean Boisselier: New Horizons, Thames and Hudson, 1994.

*Buddhists in Britain Today*, Denise Cush: Hodder & Stoughton, 1990.

*A Student's Approach to Buddhism*, Denise Cush: Hodder and
    Stoughton, 1993.
*Buddhism in the Twentieth Century*, Peggy Morgan: Hulton
    Educational, 1985.
*Being a Buddhist*, P. Morgan: Batsford, 1989.
*Buddhism*, P. and H. Connolly: Stanley Thornes, 1992.
*Teaching RE: Buddhism 5–11*: CEM.

## Christianity

*Teaching Christianity*, W. Owen Cole and Ruth Mantin:
    Heinemann, 1994.
*Christianity in Words and Pictures*, Sarah Thorley: RMEP.
*Teaching RE*: CEM, booklets on *Christmas 5–14, Easter 5–14,
    Pentecost 5–11.*
*The Many Paths of Christianity*, Jan and Mel Thompson:
    Hodder and Stoughton, 1988.
*Resource Bank: Using the Bible in the Primary Curriculum*,
    Margaret Cooling and Diane Walker with Maggie Goodwin:
    Bible Society.
*Christianity*, (Teacher's book) Westhill Project.
*Christianity: A Pictorial Guide*, CEM, 1991.
*Christmas* and *Easter*, M. Lynch: BFSS National RE Centre.
*Faith in History: Ideas for RE, History and Assembly in the
    Primary School*, Margaret Cooling: Eagle.

## Hinduism

*Hindu Children in Britain*, R. Jackson and E. Nesbitt: Trentham
    Books, 1993.
*Hinduism*, P. Bahree, Batsford, 1984.
*Approaches to Hinduism*, R. Jackson and D. Killingley: John
    Murray, 1988.
*The Mahabharata*, R. K. Narayan: Vision Books, 1987.
*Hindu Story and Symbol*, booklet by Jenny Rose: BFSS
    National RE Centre.
*Hinduism in Words and Pictures*, Sarah Thorley: Chansitor
    Publications, 1993.
*Teaching RE: Hinduism 5–11*, CEM.
*Hinduism: A Pictorial Guide*, CEM.
*Hinduism*, (Teacher's book) Westhill Project.

## Islam

*Islam*, R. James, Batsford.

*Islam wallets, Primary RE Materials*, Centre for the study of Islam and Christian-Muslim relations and the Regional RE Centre (Midlands), 1986.

*Islam in Words and Pictures*, Sarah Thorley: RMEP.

*Exploring a Theme: Islam*, CEM booklet.

*Exploring a Theme: Hajj — Pilgrimage to Mecca*, CEM.

*Islam*, (Teacher's Book) Westhill Projects.

*Islam: A Pictorial Guide*, CEM, 1991.

*Islamic Story, Folklore and Pattern*, Jenny Rose: BFSS National RE Centre.

### Judaism

*The Jewish Catalogue*, Strassfeld & Strassfeld, Jewish Education Bureau.

*Judaism*, Nicholas de Lange: OUP.

*Brainwaves: Teaching and Learning the Jewish Festivals*, Janet Mort and Linda Morris: United Synagogue Publications Ltd. 1991.

*Celebrating the Jewish Holidays*, S. Kalman and B. Mitchell: Jewish Education Bureau.

*Judaism in Words and Pictures*, Sarah Thorley: RMEP.

*Exploring a Theme: Judaism*, CEM booklet.

*Judaism*, (Teacher's book) Westhill Project.

*Judaism: A Pictorial Guide*, CEM.

*Hannukah*, L. Broadbent: BFSS National RE Centre.

*Passover*, M. Lynch: BFSS National RE Centre.

### Sikhism

*Teach Yourself Sikhism*, (Teach Yourself World Faiths Series) W. Owen Cole: Hodder and Stoughton, 1994.

*Teaching RE: Sikhism 5–11*, CEM, 1994.

*Sikhism*, Biryl Dhanjal: Batsford.

*The Sikhs in Britain*, Alan de Souza: Batsford.

*Sikhism: A Pictorial Guide*, CEM, 1991.

## Books for the classroom

### General themes

*Founders of Religions: The Buddha, Jesus Christ and Mohammed*, T. Triggs: Wayland 1981.

*Holy Cities Series*, (Rome, Jerusalem, Mecca, Varanasi, Salt Lake City, Amritsar): Evans Brothers, 1993.

*Religions Through Festivals*, (Series of 6 books) (Ed.) Clive Erricker: Longman, 1989.

*Festivals Series*, Wayland 1984/5 (Hallowe'en, Harvest and Thanksgiving, New Year, in addition to those listed below).

*Discovering Religions* (series): Heinemann, 1987.

*Celebrations* (series): Wayland, 1989. (Christmas, Easter, Hallowe'en, Harvest, New Year, Hindu festivals, Jewish festivals, Muslim festivals).

*Seasonal Festivals*, (4 books, Spring, Summer, Autumn, Winter) M. Rosen: Wayland, 1990.

*Pioneers in History*, Michael Pollard: Heinemann, 1991. (Fry, Barnardo, Schweitzer, Mother Teresa, Luther King, Desmond Tutu).

*Twenty Campaigners for Change*, Wayland.

*Profiles Series*, Hamish Hamilton, 1982–5, (Edith Cavell, Anne Frank, Basil Hume, Helen Keller, Pope John Paul II, Mother Teresa).

*Faith in Action Series*, RMEP (large number of titles).

*Great Lives* (series), Wayland (Ann Frank, Luther King, Helen Keller, Mother Teresa, Louis Braille, Florence Nightingale).

*People with a Purpose series*, SCM Press, 1973–5 (Mother Teresa, Trevor Huddleston, Helder Camara, George Macleod, Kenneth Kaunda, Barbara Ward, James Baldwin, Danilo Dolci).

*Understanding Religions Series*, Wayland, 1992 (Birth, Death, Food and Fasting, Initiation Ceremonies, Marriage Customs, Pilgrimages and Journeys).

*Discovering Sacred Texts*, (6 books in the series covering the major world religions) (Ed.) W. Owen Cole: Heinemann, 1994.

*Religions of the World*, Elizabeth Breuilly and Martin Palmer: Sainsbury–Harper Collins, 1993.

*Living Religions Project*, C. Richards (Ed.): Nelson, 1998.

## Relating to specific religions

### Buddhism

*Buddhism* (Religions of the World series), J. Snelling: Wayland, 1986.

*I am a Buddhist*, D. and U. Samarasekara: Franklin Watts, 1985.

*Buddhist Festivals*, J. Snelling: Wayland, 1985.

*Festivals of the Buddha*, A. Bancroft: RMEP, 1984.

*Buddhism*, (Religions Through Festivals series) P. and H. Connolly: Longman, 1989.

*Our Culture — Buddhist*, Jenny Wood: Franklin Watts, 1988.

*The Buddhist Experience* (Seeking Religion series), Mel Thompson: Hodder & Stoughton.

*The Buddha's Birthday* (Bridges to Religion series): Heinemann, 1994) (KS1).

*Ananada in Sri Lanka* (The Way We Are series) C. Baker: Hamish Hamilton, 1984.

*The Buddha* (Leaders of Religion series) Dilwyn Hunt: Oliver and Boyd, 1987.

*The Buddhist World* (Religions of the World series) A. Bancroft: Macdonald, 1984.

*Buddhism*, (Our World, Life and Faith series) Hulton Educational Publications Ltd., 1983.

*Our Culture: Buddhist*, Franklin Watts (series), 1988.

*Listening to Buddhists*, (series Ed.) Olivia Bennett: Unwin Hyman, 1990.


**Christianity**

*Christianity*, (Religions of the World series) Wayland, 1986.

*I am an Anglican*, M. and J. Killingray: Franklin Watts, 1986.

*I am Greek Orthodox*, M. Rossou: Franklin Watts, 1985.

*I am a Roman Catholic*, B. Pettenuzzo: Franklin Watts, 1985.

*I am a Pentecostal*, B. Pettenuzzo: Franklin Watts, 1986.

*New Baby*, J. Baskerville: A & C Black, 1985.

*Lucy's Sunday* (Bridges to Religions series) Heinemann, 1995.

*Colin's Baptism* (The Way We Are Series) O. Bennett: Hamish Hamilton, 1986.

*The Christian World*, A. Brown: Macdonald 1984.

*Visiting an Anglican Church*, S. Tompkins: Lutterworth,

*Christianity* (Religions Through Festivals series) R. O. Hughes: Longman, 1989.

*Christmas*, A. Blackwood: Wayland, 1984.

*Christmas Tinderbox*, S. Nicholls: A & C Black.

*The Lion Christmas Book*, Mary Batchelor: 1988.

*Easter*, J. Fox: Wayland, 1984.

*An Egg for Babcha* (Bridges to Religions series) Heinemann, 1995.

*We Celebrate Easter*, Bobbie Kalman: Crabtree Publishing, 1985.

*The Easter Book*, Ann Farncombe: National Christian Education Council.

*The Heroes of Christianity*, Alan Robinson (Learning about Religion series) Schofield & Sims, 1980. (St. Francis, William Booth, John Wesley, Mother Teresa, Albert Schweitzer, Elizabeth Fry).

*Christians*, John Drane: Lion, 1994.

*Jesus, the man who changed history*, John Drane: Lion

*Jesus*, (Leaders of Religion series) Oliver and Boyd, 1987.

*How the Bible Came To Us*, Meryl Doney: Lion, 1985.

*Christians 1 and 2*, Westhill Project RE 5–16.

*The Children's Illustrated Bible*, Selina Hastings: Dorling Kindersley, 1994.

*A Child's First Bible*, Stoddard/Chen: Hamlyn, 1991.

*The Puffin Children's Bible*

*Listening to Christians* (Series Ed.) Olivia Bennett: Unwin & Hyman, 1990.

*Growing up in Christianity* (series) Longman, 1990.

**Hinduism**

*Hinduism*, (Religions of the World series) Wayland, 1986.

*Hinduism* (Our World: Life and Faith series) Hulton: 1983.

*The Hindu World*, P. Bahree: Macdonald, 1982.

*Our Culture: Hindu* Franklin Watts (series) 1988.

*My Class at Diwali*, Fairclough: Franklin Watts

*Diwali*, C. Deshpande (Celebrations) A & C Black, 1994.

*I am a Hindu*, M. Aggarwal and Fairclough: Franklin Watts, 1984.

*Sweet-toothed Sunil*, J. Solomon: Hamish Hamilton

*Hinduism*, (Religions Through Festivals series) Robert Jackson: Longman, 1988.

*Hinduism*, V. P. Kanitkar: Wayland

*Hindu Festivals*, S. Mitter: Wayland, 1985.

*Wedding Day*, (The Way We Are series) J. Solomon: Hamish Hamilton, 1981.

*A Present for Mum*, (The Way We Are series) J. Solomon: Hamish Hamilton, 1981.

*Holi*, O. Bennett: Hamish Hamilton, 1987.

*Diwali*, (Celebrations series) B. Candappa: Ginn, 1985.

*Diwali*, O. Bennett: Macmillan, 1986.

*The Story of the Hindus*, Jacqueline Suthren Hirst: CUP, 1989.

*Hindus 1 and 2*, The Westhill Project RE 5–16: Stanley Thornes( Publishers) Ltd.

*Listening to Hindus*, (Series Ed.) Olivia Bennett: Unwin & Hyman, 1990.

*The Hindu Experience*, (Seeking Religion series) Liz Aylett: Hodder and Stoughton, 1992.

*Growing up in Hinduism*, J. Hirs and G. Pandey: Longman, 1990.

*Indian Food and Drink*, V. Kanitkar: Wayland, 1986.

*Dance of Shiva*, P. Mitchell: Hamish Hamilton, 1989.

*Journey with the Gods*, L. Shanson and A. Chowdry: Mantra, 1987.

## Islam

*Islam* (Religions of the World series) Wayland, 1986.

*Islam* (Our World: Life and Faith series) Hulton: 1983.

*Our Culture: Muslim*: Franklin Watts (series), 1988.

*I am a Muslim*, Aggarwal and Nazir: Franklin Watts, 1985.

*Being a Muslim*, A. Wood: Batsford, 1987.

*Something to Share* (Bridges to Religions series) Heinemann, 1995.

*Nahda's Family* (Strands series) M. Blakeley: A & C Black, 1977.

*Gifts and Almonds* (The Way We Are series), J. Solomon: Hamish Hamilton, 1980.

*The Muslim World*, Richard Tames: Macdonald, 1982.

*Eid-ul-Fitr* (Celebrations), K. McLeish: Ginn, 1985.

*Muslim Festivals*, J. Mayled: RMEP, 1990.

*Muslim Festivals*, M. M. Ahson: Wayland, 1985.

*Travellers and Explorers*: IQRA Trust, 1992.

*The Prophets*: IQRA Trust, 1992.

*Muhammad* (Leaders of Religion series) Dilwyn Hunt: Oliver & Boyd, 1985.

*Muslims 1 and 2*, The Westhill Project RE 5–16.

*Listening to Muslims* (Series Ed.) Olivia Bennett: Unwin & Hyman, 1990.

*The Muslim Experience* (Seeking Religion series) Liz Aylett: Hodder & Stoughton, 1991.

*Growing up in Islam*, Janet Ardavan: Longman, 1990.

## Judaism

*Judaism* (Religions of the World series) Wayland, 1986.

*Judaism* (Our World: Life and Faith series) Hulton, 1983.

*Our Culture: Jewish*, Jenny Woods: Franklin Watts (series), 1988.

*Judaism*, (Religions Through Festivals series) Clive Lawton: Longman, 1989.

*The Jewish World* (Religions of the World series) Douglas Charing: Macdonald, 1983.

*I am a Jew*, Clive Lawton: Franklin Watts, 1984.

*Simon, Leah and Benjamin* (Strands series) C. Knapp: A & C Black, 1979.

*Hannukka* (Celebrations series) L. Berg: Ginn, 1985.

*Mazal-Tov — A Jewish Wedding*, Jose Patterson: Hamish Hamilton, 1988.

*A Happy New Year*, Jose Patterson: Hamish Hamilton, 1987.

*Ten Good Rules*, Susan Remick Topek: Kar-Ben copies Inc., 1991.

*Matza and Bitter Herbs*, (The Way We Are series) Clive Lawton: Hamish Hamilton, 1984.

*Sam's Passover* (Celebrations), Lynne Hannigan: A & C Black, 1985.

*The Seventh Day is Shabbat* (Bridges to Religions series), Heinemann, 1995.

*The Jewish World*, D. Charing: Macdonald

*Judaism*, M. Domnitz: Wayland

*A Jewish Family in Britain*, V. Barnett: RMEP

*Jewish Festivals*, R. Turner: Wayland, 1985.

*Moses* (Leaders of Religion series) Oliver & Boyd, 1985.

*Jews 1 and 2*, The Westhill Project RE 5–16, Stanley Thornes (Publishers) Ltd., 1990.

*Listening to Jews*, (Series Ed.) Olivia Bennett: Unwin & Hyman, 1990.

*Growing up in Judaism* (series), Longman: 1990.

## Sikhism

*Sikhism* (Religions of the World series), Wayland: 1986.

*Our Culture: Sikh*: Franklin Watts (series), 1988.

*I am a Sikh*, M. Aggarwal: Franklin Watts, 1984.

*Pavan is a Sikh* (Strands series), Sean Lyle: A & C Black, 1977.

*A Sikh Wedding* (The Way We Are series), O. Bennett: Hamish Hamilton, 1987.

*Kilkar's Drum* (The Way We Are series), O. Bennett: Hamish Hamilton, 1984.

*Bobbi's New Year*, (The Way We Are series), J. Solomon: Hamish Hamilton, 1980.

*News for Dad*, (The Way We Are series), J. Solomon: Hamish Hamilton, 1980.

*Baisakhi Book*, Multicultural Education Centre, Bishops Road, Bristol

*Listening to Sikhs*, (Series Ed.) Olivia Bennett: Unwin & Hyman, 1990.

*Growing up in Sikhism*, Andrew Clutterbuck: Longman, 1990.

*The Sikh World*, (Religions of the World series), D. Singh and A. Smith: Macdonald, 1985.

*Sikhism*, (Religions Through Festivals series), Davinder Kaur Babraa: Longman, 1989.

*Sikh Festivals*, S Kapoor: Wayland, 1985.


## Stories

### Multi-faith stories/myths and legends

*The Green Umbrella*, Jill Brand, Wendy Blows and Caroline Short: WWF/A & C Black, 1991.

*Out of the Ark; Stories from the World's Religions*, Anita Ganeri: Simon and Schuster Young Books.

*Worlds of Difference* (Creation Stories), Martin Palmer and Esther Bisset: WWF/Blackie, 1989.

*Creation Stories*, M Lynch: BFSS National RE Centre.

*Creation Stories*, (Religious Stories series) Wayland, 1987.

*Chinese Stories*, (Religious Stories series) Wayland, 1987.

*Faith Stories for Today*, Angela Wood: BBC/Longman. (10 stories)

*Sunshine Religious Stories*, (12 stories covering the 6 major faiths) Heinemann, 1995).

*Heroes of the Faiths; Assembly Stories from around the World*, (Buddhist, Chinese, Hindu, Jewish, Muslim, Sikh, Christian), William Dargue: OUP, 1985.

*A Tapestry of Tales*, Sandra Palmer and Elizabeth Breuilly.

*Realms of Gold*, (Myths and Legends from around the World), Ann Pilling: Kingfisher, 1993.

*The Myth of Isis and Osiris*, Jules Cashford: Barefoot Books, 1993.

*Theseus and the Minotaur*, Jules Cashford: Barefoot Books, 1995.

*The Wizard Punchkin* (Folk Tales of the World series) Joanna Troughton: Puffin.

*Tortoise's Dream* (Folk Tales of the World series) Joanna Troughton: Puffin.

*How Rabbit Stole the Fire*, Joanna Troughton: Penguin.

*What Made Tiddalick Laugh*, Joanna Troughton: Penguin.

*Salt is Sweeter than Gold*, Andrew Peters: Barefoot Books, 1994.

*The Birds Who Flew Beyond Time*, Ann Baring and Thetis Blacker: Barefoot Books, 1993.

*The Dragon's Pearl*, retold by Julie Lawson: OUP, 1992.

*Alan Garner's Book of British Fairy Tales*, Collins, 1984.

*Whales Canoe*, Joanna Troughton: Blackie, 1993.

*African Stories* and *Native North American Stories*, Robert Hull: Wayland, 1992.

**Buddhist**

*Buddhist Stories*, John Snelling: Wayland, 1986.

*The Buddha and the Elephant*, (Multi-faith Fables), Mary Glasgow Publications, 1989.

*Prince Siddhartha*, J. Landaw and J. Brooke: Wisdom, 1990.

*The Mountains of Tibet*, Mordicai Gerstein: Barefoot Books, 1987.

*The Life of the Buddha*, (Religious Stories series) John Snelling: Wayland, 1987.

*Jataka Tales: Golden Foot, Heart of Gold, A Precious Life*, Dharma Publishing (available through Windhorse Publications).

**Christian**

*Stories from the Christian World*, D. Self: Macdonald.

*The Story of Jesus*, Mary Batchelor: Lion, 1992.

*The Bible in 365 Stories*, Mary Batchelor: Lion.

*The Life of Jesus* (Religious Stories series) Wayland,

*Old Testament Stories* (Religious Stories series) Wayland.

*Bible Stories for Classroom and Assembly*, (separate OT/NT), Jack Priestley: RMEP 1992.

*What the Bible Tells Us* series, The Bible Societies, 1977.

*The Lives of the Saints* (Religious Stories series) N. Martin: Wayland, 1986.

*Stories Jesus Told* (series), Nick Butterworth and Mick Inkpen: Collins Picture Lions, 1989.

*Stories from the Bible*, (OT stories), Martin Waddell: Francis Lincoln Ltd., 1993.

*A First Puffin Picture Book of Bible Stories*, Annabel Shilson-Thomas, 1994.

*The Life of Jesus* (Story Readers) Sue Goodwin: Hodder & Stoughton, 1990, (stories, notes for teachers, worksheets).

*People of the Bible: The Bible Through Stories and Pictures*, retold by Catherine Storr: Franklin Watts, 1986.

*Tomie de Paola's Book of Bible Stories*, Tomie de Paola: Hodder and Stoughton, 1990.

*The Bible Storybook*, Georgie Adams: Orion, 1994.

*Tales of Heaven and Earth: Sarah who Loved Laughing*: Moonlight Publishing, 1994.

*The Road to Bethlehem: A Nativity Story from Ethiopia*, told by Elizabeth Laird: William Collins Sons and Co., 1987.

*A Lion for the King, A Christmas Legend from the Orient*, retold by Meryl Doney, Lion.

*Baboushka*, Lion.

*The Singing Shepherd*, Angela Elwell Hunt: Lion, 1992.

*Caspar and the Star*, Francesca Bosca: Lion.

*Story of the Three Wise Kings*, Tomie de Paola: Methuen, 1985.

*Jesus' Christmas Party*, Nicholas Alan: Hutchinson, 1991.

*Christmas*, Jan Pienkowski: Heinemann.

*Bring in the Holly*, (12 poems), Charles Causley: Frances Lincoln.

*Mary Jones and her Bible*, Mig Holder: Bible Society, 1992.

*St. Francis of Assisi*, Nina Bawden: Jonathan Cape, 1983.

*St. Francis, The Birds and the Wolf*, (Multi-faith Fables) Mary Glasgow Publications, 1989.

*How St. Francis Tamed the Wolf*, Elizabeth Rose: Bodley Head, 1982.

*The Easter Story*, Brian Wildsmith: OUP.

*Easter*, Jan Pienkowski: Heinemann, 1989.

## Hindu

*Seasons of Splendour*, Madhur Jaffrey: Pavilion Books, 1992.

*The Indian Story Book*, R. Singh: Heinemann.

*Hindu Stories* (Religious Stories series) V. P. (Hemant) Kanitkar: Wayland.

*Stories from the Hindu World*, Jamila Gavin, Macdonald.

*The Story of Prince Ram*, R. Singh: BBC.

*The Story of Prince Rama*, B. Thompson: Kestrel, 1980.

*Rama and Sita* (Folktales of the World) Gorinder Ram: Blackie.

*Tales of Heaven and Earth; The River Goddess*: Moonlight Publishing, 1994.

*Hanuman the Mighty Monkey*, Barefoot Books.

*Hanuman*, A. Ramachandran: A & C Black, 1979.

*The Mouse and the Doves*, (Multi-faith Fables) Mary Glasgow Publications, 1989.

*Chavitri*, Aaron Shephard: Albert Witman & Co., 1993, available from Letterbox Library.

*The Butter Thief*, Chris Murray: The Bhaktivedanta Book Trust, 1991.

*Citylinks Series* (6 stories about Hindu life in Britain), June Jones: Blackie, 1987.

**Jewish**

*Stories from the Jewish World*, Sybil Sheridan: Macdonald.

*Jewish Tales*, Leo Paulac: Jewish Education Bureau.

*Just enough is Plenty*, Barbara Goldin: Heinemann, 1988.

*Hannukah*, Roni Schotter: Joy Street Books, Little Brown and Co., 1990.

*A Family Hannukah*, Bobbi Katz: Random House, available from Jewish Education Bureau.

*Hannukah*, Jenny Koralek: Walker Books, 1992.

*Saul and the Donkeys*, (Multi-faith Fables) Mary Glasgow Publications, 1989.

*Daddy's Chair*, Sandy Lanton: Karben Copies (available from Jewish Education Bureau).

**Muslim**

*Stories from the Muslim World*, Huda Khattab: Macdonald.

*Stories of the Prophets of Islam from Adam to Hud*, Abdul Rahman Rukaini, Macmillan.

*Stories of the Prophets of Islam — Musa*, Abdul Rahman Rukaini, Macmillan.

*The Life of Muhammad* (Religious Stories series) Maryan Davies, Wayland.

*Tales of Heaven and Earth: I want to talk to God*: Moonlight Publishing, 1994.

*The Cat and the Dog* (Multi-faith Fables) Mary Glasgow Publications, 1989.

*The Wonderful Bag*, Gini Ward: Blackie.
*Citylinks Series*, (6 stories about Muslim life in Britain), June
    Jones: Blackie, 1987.

### Sikh

*Stories from the Sikh World*, R. and J. Singh: Macdonald.
*Guru Nanak and the Sikh Gurus*, Ranjit Arora: Wayland, 1987.
*Nanak, the Cattle and the Cobra* (Multi-faith Fables) Mary
    Glasgow Publications, 1989.

## Appropriate themes in secular stories

Some of these stories have been grouped according to theme,
but this is only intended to be a rough guide as stories may
have more than one theme.

Refer also to *Tell Me a Story*, M. Lynch, BFSS National RE
Centre (annotated selection of stories for RE, arranged
thematically).

### Alter ego/Accepting responsibility

*Oscar Got the Blame*, Tony Ross: Red Fox, 1991.

### Death/funerals/bereavement

*Fred*, Posy Simmonds: Picture Puffins, 1989.
*Granpa*, John Burningham: Picture Puffins, 1988.
*Badger's Parting Gifts*, Susan Varley: Picture Lions, 1984.
*Remembering Mum*, Ginny Perkins and Leon Morris: A & C
    Black, 1991.
*Kirsty's Kite*, Carol Curtis Stilz, Albatross.
*I'll Always Love You*, H. Wilhelm: Hodder, 1985.
*John's Book*, Jill Fuller: Lutterworth Press, 1993.
*Mama's Going To Buy You A Mocking Bird*, J. Little: Puffin,
    1985.

### Dream/reality: Endangered world

*The Whale's Song*, Dyan Sheldon and Gary Blythe: Red Fox,
    1993.
*Oi! Get Off Our Train*, John Burningham: Jonathan Cape, 1992.

## Different viewpoints

*The Same But Different*, Tessa Dahl: Picture Puffins, 1990.
*Once There Were Giants*, Martin Waddell: Walker, 1989.
*Carry Go Bring Come*, Vynne Samuels: Red Fox, 1988.

## Family bonds across time and space

*From Me To You*, Paul Rogers: Orchard, 1987.
*A Balloon for Grandad*, Nigel Gray: Picture Lions, 1990.
*Emerald Blue*, Ann Marie Linden: Heinemann, 1995.
*Granny's Quilt*, Penny Ives: Puffin, 1995.

## Family and home

*Jack and the Monster*, Richard Graham and Susan Varley: Red
    Fox, 1990.
*Changes*, Anthony Browne: Julia MacRae Books, 1990.
*Kids*, Catherine and Laurence Anholt: Walker Books, 1992.
*Not Now Bernard*, David McKee: Red Fox, 1991.
*Why Do You Love Me*? Walker, 1990.

## Fears/uncertainties

*There's An Alligator Under My Bed*, Mercer Mayer: MacMillan,
    1987.
*Alfie Gives a Hand*, Shirley Hughes: Picture Lions, 1985.
*Don't Forget To Write*, Martina Selway: Hutchinson, 1991.
*Angelmae*, Shirley Hughes? Walker
*I Won't Go There Again*, Susan Hill: Walker, 1991.

## Feelings

*Good Days, Bad Days*, Catherine Anholt: Orchard Picturebooks,
    1993.
*Angry Arthur*, Hiawyn Oram: Red Fox, 1993.
*Teacher's Pet*, Nicola Smee: Picture Lions, 1993.
*The Big, Big Sea*, Martin Waddell: Walker Books, 1995.

## Friends/relationships/ behaviour

*Manners*, Aliki: Little Mammoth, 1992.
*Bailey the Big Bully*, Anthony Browne
*A Pig Called Shrimp*, Lisa Taylor: Harper Collins
*The Bully*, Jan Needle: Puffin, 1995.
*The Bullies Meet the Willow Street Kids*, Michele Elliott:
　　Piccolo, 1993.
*The Present Takers*, Aidan Chambers
*Chris and the Dragon*, Fay Sampson: Puffin

## Individual worth/self-esteem

*I Wish I Could Fly*, Ron Maris: Julia MacRae, 1986.
*Ruby*, Maggie Glenn: Hutchinson, 1990.
*Nancy No-Size*, Mary Hoffman and Jennifer Northway: Little
　　Mammoth, 1991.
*Something Special*, David McPhail: Penguin
*Me Too*, Susan Winter: Dorling Kindersley

## Love/jealousy/sharing

*John Brown, Rose and the Midnight Cat*, Jenny Wagner: Picture
　　Puffin, 1979.
*Black Dog*, Pamela Allen: Picture Puffin, 1991.

## Moving home

*Monty's Journey*, Paul Geraghty: Picture Lions.
*Moving*, Michael Rosen: Viking.

## Parental separation

*Where Has Daddy Gone?*, Trudy Osman: Mammoth, 1994.
*Are We Nearly There?*, Louis Baum: Bodley Head

## Personal possessions

*Polly's Puffin*, Sarah Garland: Picture Puffin, 1990.
*Dogger*, Shirley Hughes: Red Fox, 1993.

## Priorities/values

*Herbert and Harry*, Pamela Allen: Picture Puffin, 1991.
*The Selfish Giant*, O. Wilde: Picture Puffin, 1978.

## Transformation/mystery

*Gorilla*, Anthony Browne: Julia MacRae Books, 1983.
*The Velveteen Rabbit*, M. Williams, Heinemann, 1983.

## War/prejudice

*Tusk Tusk*, David McKee: Beaver Books, 1988.

## Youth and age

*Wilfrid Gordon McDonald Partridge*, Mem Fox: Picture Puffins, 1984.
*Grandpa and Me*, M. Alex and B. Alex: Lion, 1983.
*Taro and his Grandmother*, H. East: Macdonald, 1986.
*Not So Fast Songolo*, Niki Daly: Puffin, 1987.

## Others

*Stories by Firelight*, Shirley Hughes: Bodley Head, 1993.
*Fantastic Stories*, Terry Jones: Pavilion, (1992 rep. 1993).
*The Willow Street Kids*, Michele Elliott: Piccolo, 1986.
*The Moon Lady*, Amy Tan: Puffin, 1992.
*The Cherry Tree*, Brian Wildsmith: OUP, 1991.
*A New Coat for Anna*, Harriet Ziefert: Julia MacRae/Franklin Watts, 1986.
*Charlotte's Web*, E. B. White: Puffin, 1963.
*The Lion, the Witch and the Wardrobe*, C. S. Lewis, Puffin.
*The Iron Man*, Ted Hughes, Puffin.
*Goodnight Mr. Tom*, Michelle Magorian: Puffin, 1981.
*Shine*, Jill Paton Walsh: Macdonald, 1981.
*The Secret Garden*, Frances Hodgson Burnett: Puffin, 1951.
*The Mouse and His Child*, R. Hoban: Faber & Faber, 1969.
*How The Whale Became & Other Stories*, Ted Hughes: Puffin, 1963.

The large part of this bibliography was compiled by Mrs C. Gravestock, Research Assistant at the University of Brighton as part of the RE Coordinators Project.

## Artefacts

Artefacts have over past years assumed an important place in RE teaching. Artefacts are essentially objects which are used in worship and although in the classroom they are removed from their actual use, they can be very powerful agents in assisting pupils to understand religious traditions more effectively. Teachers will use them in different ways, perhaps as a stimulus or as reinforcement in teaching, but they do have the strengths of being first hand experience, tangible and also there! Videos can break down but artefacts are invariably reliable.

Artefacts can be expensive so they will need to be chosen with care and this is one of the advantages of having a clear scheme of work — it is possible to acquire those which support the areas being taught. If funding is a serious problem then a good 'second best' is to make some. One school made Buddhist prayer wheels in Year 5 (actually as a design and technology task); another school had children making a Torah scroll.

There is a concern among some teachers that they might be causing offence unwittingly by an insensitive use of artefacts. Although as a general point if artefacts are handled and treated with respect, there is unlikely to be any affront caused, there are some specific points which are worth noting. For example: only handle a copy of the Qur'an with clean hands, keep it from contact with dirty floors and when it is not in use keep it wrapped in a clean cloth, again away from the floor; tell pupils not to touch the Torah scrolls on a synagogue visit and display tefellin in a box and do not handle; in a Hindu mandir, pupils should be told not to attempt to touch the murti. Very useful guidance on the detailed use of artefacts in the classroom can be found in *Religious Artefacts in the Classroom*, P. Gateshill and J. Thompson, Hodder and Stoughton, 1995.

Schools naturally organise their artefact resources in different ways. An effective way is to have the supply of artefacts stored carefully in a cupboard and to have lists of artefacts suitable for different parts of RE teaching. As a number of artefacts can be used in different topics then a teacher can go to the cache of artefacts and select the appropriate ones for the particular piece of RE teaching and so make up, for example, a Divali box or a mosque box.

Artefacts can be purchased probably most cheaply in shops which serve members of the different religious traditions and this is an option for those who have easy access to these. There are also a number of agencies which supply artefacts for educational purposes. Notable among these are:

| **Articles of Faith** | **Religion in Evidence** |
|---|---|
| Bury Business Centre | TTS, Monk Road |
| Kay Street | Alfreton |
| Bury BL9 6BU | Derbyshire DE55 7RL |

## Basic artefact collections

A full collection of artefacts for a religious tradition would be almost endless; below are listed some of the key artefacts which are most appropriate to areas of work normally covered in primary schools.

### Christianity

| | |
|---|---|
| Cross | candles (votive, baptismal, Paschal) |
| Crucifix | palm cross |
| Bible (various versions) | rosary |
| Icon(s) | chalice, paten and wafers |
| small statues | Advent calendar and candle |
| (e.g. Virgin and Child) | stole |

### Buddhism

| | |
|---|---|
| Statue of the Buddha | Prayer wheel |

### Hinduism

Murtis (e.g. Rama & Sita, Krishna, Vishnu, Shiva, Lakshmi, Ganesh)

Puja tray     Divas
Arti lamp     Garlands
Divali cards

## Islam

Qu'ran and cover    compass
Qur'an stand    Prayer beads
Prayer mat    calligraphy plaques

## Judaism

Tallith (prayer shawl)    Seder plate
Yamulka (prayer hat)    Menorah/Hanukkiah
Torah scroll (small)    Havdalah candle
Yad (pointer)    Matzos
Mezuzah    Festival cards
Sabbath candlesticks

## Sikhism

Kara (bangle)    Turban length
Kangha (comb)    Chauri
Kirpan (dagger)    Rumala (covering cloth for the Guru Granth
Turban    Sahib)

# Posters/photopacks

*Westhill Project Photopacks* accompany their other material on the major world religions. They are durable, include detailed information on the back of each picture and teachers' booklets.

*Pictorial Charts Educational Trust* produces posters on a wide variety of RE themes (e.g. Creation Stories, Birth Rites, Marriage Rites, Festivals, Holy Places, Five Pillars of Islam, The Hajj, Hindu Gods, Religious Artefacts).

*CEM posters*: Jesus Worldwide, Christmas posters, Easter posters.

Picture materials relating to RE themes can also be found in periodicals for primary teachers e.g. *Child Education, Junior Education* and *Infant Projects*.

## Videos

*Schools' Television*:

*Coming Together* and *Movable Feasts* are both aimed at
children in the primary age range and deal with the major
world religions. There are notes to accompany the series.
Cross-curricular series such as *Watch* (Light across the
Faiths, Christmas: Nativity; Food and Fasting) and *All
Year Round* (Death, New Life) also treat RE themes. Some
topics in the Central TV. *Believe it or Not* series (lower
secondary) may also be useful for older juniors e.g. The
Hajj: Pilgrimage to Makkah.

*CEM videos*, (PEP), particularly *Living Festivals* (Chanukah,
Christmas, Chinese New Year, Pesach, Easter, Succot,
Divali, Guru Nanak's Birthday) and *Looking at Faith*
(multi-faith) with notes for teachers and pupils.

*Buddhism in KS2 video pack* with notes and worksheets
(sections on The Buddha, The Dharma, The Sangha,
Meditation and Worship), Clear Vision Trust.

## RE and ICT

As information and communications technology becomes
increasingly significant in the school curriculum, so RE too
will make use of this powerful aid to learning. Particularly
appropriate ways of helping pupils to understand religious
traditions more effectively can be enhanced in the following
ways:

- communicating information — modifying and presenting
  information in a number of ways using numbers, pictures
  and words;
- handling information — storing, retrieving and presenting
  information;
- modelling — using simulations of events to identify
  changes and trends.

Software usually comes in one of the following three formats:
- floppy disc
- CD-ROM (Compact Disc Read Only Memory)
- through the Internet and the World Wide Web (WWW).

There is as yet only a limited number of RE specific programmes but others can also have an applicable RE content. RE coordinators are advised to discuss possibilities with their school's ICT coordinator. The following organisation can also be a valuable source of help:

NCET
Milburn Hill Road,
Science Park
Coventry CV4 7JJ

## Chapter 12

Visits and visitors

## Visiting religious buildings

All religions express themselves in buildings and it is in these buildings that the faithful believe that in some special way they meet with the divine. There, too, various significant rituals take place, festivals are celebrated and special objects or artefacts are housed for example, the altar in a church, the murti in a mandir, the Ark in a synagogue and so on. To try to understand any religion without experiencing its place of worship is very difficult if not impossible. To try to experience it additionally as a *living* centre is infinitely preferable though not always possible in the working week.

There can be few schools which are not within walking distance of a church, whether it be the village church, a town church on the corner or a cathedral. Many, too, will also have access to synagogues, mosques and temples/mandirs. A place of worship is an extremely important resource in RE — children find their visits so memorable — yet it is one which is often neglected.

Visiting places of worship is extremely time consuming both in the teacher's time in making the arrangements and in the pupils' time out of school so it is therefore important that visits are planned carefully and are integral to the effective teaching of a unit of RE. Generally visits to places of worship can have two main purposes, cognitive and affective:

> *Cognitive*: pupils will be able to see the objects of worship and identify them and also to understand something of their significance in the practice of the religion.
>
> *affective*: the atmosphere of a place of worship can 'speak' to the feelings. Many people who visit churches say that in some they feel a sense of peace or tranquillity, in others they have feelings of timelessness or eternity.

Visitors to Durham Cathedral often claim that it speaks to them of majesty and power, to Chartres Cathedral of mystery and depth. Some buildings do speak to people at a level deeper than that of conscious thought and it is this experience which can be very important for children. This is equally true of places of worship in other religious traditions.

Below are three comments by RE coordinators which all speak for themselves about visits to places of worship:

> Year 5 went to visit the parish church last week but as far as I can tell, nothing they did was really relevant to RE! They sketched the shape of the windows and their tracery, they rubbed gravestones, wall memorial tablets and pew ends, they calculated the height of the tower and they counted the different varieties of wild flowers in the churchyard — nothing about religion at all.

> I swear by visits to places of worship. The children love them and they remember so much about them — even the details of stained glass windows seen two years ago! I make sure that each age group makes a visit to a place of worship every year — each one with its own purpose and these are progressive.

> I took the Year 1 children to the Hindu temple at Divali time. It was full of blazing candles. The temple looked so beautiful with the images all around and the masses of candles. The children were absolutely thrilled, so excited that they were bubbling over. Their stories and their pictures afterwards were a joy to see. When I described the visit at an RE meeting at the Teachers' Centre, I received a very poor reception: what a waste of time, the children couldn't possibly understand Hinduism! What they couldn't seem to understand was that I was concerned to foster religious feeling and experience not cognitive knowledge!

## A visit to a church at Key Stage 2

Here is a visit to the parish church made by Year 2 children as part of their work on places of worship.

**Outside the church**
Look at the architecture. How do we know it is a church?
Look for clues. How old is the building? Are there any special features, signs and symbols? Is there a graveyard? Why do you think older churches often have graveyards?

**Inside the church**
First let the children 'get the feel' of the church. Sit them down quietly and get them to close their eyes.
What do they feel? Smell? Hear?
What can they see? Look at the colours, the light, the shape, the textures.
What do they like/dislike about a church.
Look at the architecture. How do you know it is a church?
Look for clues. Look at the furniture — the font, pulpit, lectern, altar, pews, organ — mark them on the worksheet.
Are there any artefacts or special objects — statues, pictures, crucifixes, crosses, candles. Why do you think they are there? What do you think they mean to people?
Look at the windows. What stories do the stained glass windows represent?
Find the church notice board. What activities does it have? Look for clues? Are there any Brownies, Guides, Cubs or Scouts?

This is only one approach but it has the virtue of focusing upon religious concerns and of encouraging critical thought through the use of questions.

## Visitors

A very useful source of first hand experience in RE for pupils can be the visitor. Appropriate visitors could be adherents of different religious traditions, clerical or lay, or possibly representatives of different aid organisations, such as Christian Aid. One school invited the priest organiser of a local church-based night shelter to speak to its Year 3/4 children about his work and its relationship to his faith. This experience, carefully prepared for, had a considerable impact on the pupils who wished afterwards to make regular collections of food, clothes and blankets for the shelter. The visit of the speaker made the work on the night shelter come alive to the pupils. In class the teacher had been able to discuss issues of homelessness and poverty and had considered in this context the work of Mother Teresa in Calcutta and also of others on a more local scale. It was the visitor who was able to come in and fire the children's imagination. This example highlights some important points about visitors to the school or the classroom which might well be borne in mind.

Firstly, it is very important that the visit is worthwhile and that it makes an important contribution to the children's learning. Arranging visits is a very time consuming activity both for the teacher who undertakes it, the visitor who comes and for the pupils for whom the experience is intended. The visitor should therefore make a contribution which the teacher is unable to make.

Secondly, it is important that the visitor is a suitable person for the task in hand. The priest organiser of the night shelter is a lively speaker who is able to communicate effectively with children and it is these two qualities which made his visit to the school so successful. Not all potential visitors are so well gifted so teachers would be well advised to check this beforehand. Local clergy may, for example, be seen as the most obvious representatives of the local Christian community but this does not necessarily mean that they are the most suitable people to visit the school to talk about what it means to be a Christian. Some most certainly will be, but it is wise to make enquiries first. Many schools have tales to tell! One school always invites in a retired teacher who is a churchwarden: she brings with her the experience of the Christian local community together with a lifetime's experience of teaching children. Other schools make use of suitable parents. One school serving a multi-faith area regularly invites parents from different religious groups in to explain major festivals in their traditions as they come round: a Muslim parent would, for example, explain what happens in a Muslim household at Eid, a Jewish parent about Passover and so on. Parents are a valuable resource often forgotten by schools. Contributions like these from visitors should not be seen as substitutes for normal RE teaching in the school but more as additions which contribute to a more personal and affective dimension of the work.

Thirdly, it is very important that visitors are clear about their brief. This means that when the arrangement is made the teacher needs to explain carefully the nature of the RE work and exactly how the visitor's contribution fits into the overall scheme. This should result in the minimum of duplication and mean that the pupils will receive the full benefit of the special contribution to the learning that the visitor is able to make.

Fourthly, it is very important that the pupils should be prepared for any visit that has been arranged. It is particularly useful if the work the children are doing in class can build up to the visit so that it is seen as something special. One school had the privilege of a visit by two Buddhist monks and a Buddhist nun. There was considerable preparation for this so that when the visit took place there was an atmosphere of excited anticipation. Pupils had learned something of Buddhism particularly with reference to the life of monks and nuns, their appearance, their chanting and so on. The visit fulfilled all expectations and everyone was delighted with the experience. However the headteacher of a nearby school, on hearing of the Buddhist visit, asked if they could visit his school for a short time after the completion of their visit to the first school. This visit was a disaster. The pupils in the second school, without any preparation for the visit, found the appearance of the visitors with their saffron robes and their shaved heads bizarre — and amusing — and the chanting which was performed for them evoked embarrassed laughter. Far from encouraging understanding and tolerance, this experience reinforced negative stereotypes.

The RE coordinator has a particular role, therefore, in identifying and making up a list of possible visitors. This list can be drawn up from information gained from colleagues in other schools, from RE advisers and advisory teachers, from staff at RE resource centres and from the faith communities themselves and should relate to the nature of RE in the school; there is little point in identifying, for example, possible Sikh speakers if Sikhism does not figure in the school RE programme.

The RE coordinator should provide guidelines for staff on the role of visitors as outlined above with additional guidance as to different cultural mores of visitors from different groups for example, it is inappropriate for a man to shake hands with a Sikh woman or an orthodox Muslim man would not normally shake hands with a woman. When offering refreshments, it is wise to bear in mind dietary rules for different groups.

Other issues to bear in mind are expenses — some do have to make a charge even if only to cover expenses — letters of thanks which, if possible should be written by children and the difficult question of whether parents ought to be informed of the contribution of proposed visitors. One rural Church of England primary school invited a representative of another religion to come to talk to the children. Parents learned about this coming visit from conversations with their children and a number wrote to the school requesting that their children should be withdrawn from the session. Such was the number that wished this that the school felt that it would have to take the embarrassing course of cancelling, or at least postponing, the session. After a meeting in which the school staff was able to convince the parents that there was no intention to try to convert the pupils to this other religion and that the aims of the enterprise were entirely educational, all the parents withdrew their objections and the visitor came at a later date. It might, however, be useful to have explained the purpose of the visitor's contribution beforehand to the parents, perhaps in the regular newsletter which is sent home.

Because a well planned and focused contribution from a visitor can be such an important addition to work in RE, a number of schools build visitors into their programmes.

---

The RE coordinator in an infant school describes her school's approach to visitors:

In our school we take RE seriously but we are aware how little time we can give to it — only 35 hours a year — because of the demands of all the subjects in the National Curriculum. We therefore are very concerned not to waste any time and not to do anything which would lead to that. We do find that visitors can make a unique contribution to aspects of our work and we do build in two every year. We focus on two religions over Key Stage 1, Christianity and Judaism so most of our RE work draws on these two traditions. In Year 1 we work on the theme of 'Babies' in the Autumn term which leads up very nicely to Christmas. Part of our RE work arising from 'Babies' concerns naming ceremonies especially baptism and every year Father Andrew from the parish church comes in to talk to the children about baptism. Before he comes the children dress up a doll in a christening robe, prepare a bowl of water for the font and light a candle. When Father Andrew arrives he tells the children stories about baptism, chooses different children to be parents and god parents, and then baptises the doll. The children thoroughly enjoy this, it makes baptism come alive and I know they remember it for a long time.

In Year 2 we do a topic on 'Food' in the Spring term. Part of the RE aspects of the topic focuses upon special foods and the significance of sharing a meal with people. Here we are very fortunate in having in the area a Jewish mother whose children used to attend the school when they were younger. Every year she comes into school to talk about the Sabbath meal shared on the Friday evening at the beginning of the Sabbath. She brings with her the candlesticks, the cloths, the bread, the wine and lays out the table for them. All the time too she emphasises the importance of the whole family gathering together to share the meal and how it welds them together. As with Father Andrew the children find this a memorable occasion and it is not one which we as teachers could do nearly so well.

I do think we are fortunate in having two willing visitors both of whom have such good rapport with the children. We are dreading the day when Father Andrew moves on; the Rector would not be half so good!

| Chapter 13 | Some useful addresses |
| --- | --- |

## Some main organisations

**Buddhist Society**
58 Ecclestone Square
London
SW1V 1PH

**Christian Education Movement**
Royal Buildings
Victoria Street
Derby DE1 1GW

**Institute of Jewish Education (IJE)**
44a Albert Road
London
NW4 2SG

**Muslim Education Trust**
130 Stroud Green Road
London
N4 3RZ

**National Christian Education Council (NCEC)**
Robert Denholm House
Nutfield
Redhill
RH1 4HW

**Professional Council for Religious Education**
Lancaster House Borough Road
Isleworth
Middlesex
TW7 5DU

**Religious Education Council for England and Wales**
CEM/Royal Buildings
Victoria Street
Derby DE1 1GW

## Major RE resource centres

**The National Society's RE Centre**
36 Causton Street
LONDON SWIP 4AU

**The York RE Centre**
The College
Lord Mayor's Walk
YORK YO3 7EX

**The BFSS National RE Centre**
Brunel University College
Osterley Campus
Borough Road
ISLEWORTH
Middlesex TW7 5DU

**The Westhill RE Centre**
Westhill College
Selly Oak
BIRMINGHAM B29 6LL

**Welsh National Centre for Religious Education Canolfan Genedlaethol Addysg Grefyddol**
School of Eucation
UCNW
Ffordd Deiniol
BANGOR
Gwynedd
Wales
LL57 2UW

## Publishers of RE material

**Folens Publishers**
Albert House
Apex Business Centre
Boscombe Road
DUNSTABLE
LU5 4RL

**Heinemann Educational Publishers**
Halley Court
Jordan Hill
OXFORD
OX2 8EJ

**Lion Publishing PLC**
Sandy Lane West
OXFORD
OX4 5HG

**Longman Group Limited**
Longman House
Burnt Mill
HARLOW
Essex
CM20 2JE

**Wayland Publishers Limited**
61 Western Road
HOVE
East Sussex
BN3 1JD

**REMP/Pergamon**
St Mary's Works
St Mary's Plain
NORWICH
NR3 3BH

**Christian Education Movement**
Royal Buildings
Victoria Street
DERBY
DE1 1GW

**Shap Working Party**
c/o The National Society's
RE Centre
36 Causton Street
LONDON SW1P 4AU

## Posters, wallcharts and artefacts

**The Westhill Project**
Westhill RE Centre
Westhill College, Selly Oak,
BIRMINGHAM B29 6LL
Poster packs on all the major world faiths.

**Pictorial Charts Educational Trust**
PCET, 27 Kirchen Road
LONDON, W13 0UD
Tel: 0181 567 9206
A wide variety of pictures, posters and wallcharts.

**Philip Green Educational Limited**
PGE, 112a Alcester Road
STUDLEY
Warwickshire BV80 7NR
Picture packs, slide-sets and filmstrips

**Folens Publishers**
Albert House, Apex Business Centre
Boscombe Road
DUNSTABLE LU5 4RL
Photopacks and posterpacks. Brochure available

**Christian Education Movement**
Royal Buildings
Victoria Street
DERBY DE3 1GW
A comprehensive collection of booklets and posters. Brochure available

**The Islamic Cultural Centre and London Central Mosque**
146 Park Road
LONDON NW8 7RG
Muslim artefacts and other resources

**ISKON Educational Services**
Bhativedanta Manor
Letchmore Heath
WATFORD
Herts WD2A 8EP
Hindu artefacts and other resources

**Gohil Emporium**
381 Stratford Road
Sparkhill
BIRMINGHAM B11 4JZ
Religious artefacts from India

**Degh Tegh Fateh**
117 Soho Road
Handsworth
BIRMINGHAM B21 9ST
All kinds of Sikh religious artefacts, books & audio visual resources.

**Religion in Evidence**
TTS
Monk Road
ALFRETON
Derbyshire DE55 7RL
Tel: 01773 830255
Religious artefacts & posters

**Articles of Faith**
Bury Business Centre
Kay Street
BURY
Lancs BL9 6BU
Tel: 0161 763 6232
Religious artefacts for all the major world faiths.

**The Jewish Education Bureau**
8 Westcombe Avenue
LEEDS LS8 2BS
Tel: 0113 293 3523

**Minaret House**
9 Leslie Park Road
CROYDON
Surrey CR0 6TN
Tel: 0181 681 2972
Muslim materials

**St Paul Multi Media Centre**
199 Kensington High Street
London W8 6BA
Tel: 0171 937 9591
A wide range of Christian materials

**The Buddhist Society**
58 Eccleston Square
London SW1V 1PH
Tel: 0171 834 5858
Wide selection of audio tapes for purchase.

**Little India**
91 The Broadway
SOUTHALL
Middlesex UB1 1LN
Hindu, Sikh and Muslim artefacts

# Index

Accountability 117
Agreed syllabuses 21, 25, 35,
     37–9, 40, 41, 42, 43, 68, 73,
     81–3, 85, 86, 95, 96, 114, 117
Aims of RE 7, 45–56
   confessional approach 46, 48,
     49, 50, 82
   factual approach 47, 50
   understanding approach 47, 51
   personal search 52
   learning about religion 23, 47,
     52–3, 82, 83, 84
   learning from religion 23, 47,
     52–3, 82, 83, 84
Artefacts 26, 27, 66–7, 123,
     139–41, 154–6
   basic collections 140–1
Assessment 23, 24, 111–15

Balance 84
Baptist Union 41
Basic Curriculum 8, 36, 62
Books for the classroom
   General themes 125–6
   Relating to specific religions
     126–31
   Stories — multifaith 131–2
     from specific religions
     128–35

Themes from secular stories
     135–8
Books for Teachers
   Festivals 122–3
   General themes 123
   Teachng RE 121
   Using artefacts 123
   World Religions 122, 123–5
British Humanist Association 48
Buddhism (Buddhists) 39, 41, 148
   Books on 123–4, 126–7
   Stories from 132

Christianity 9, 13, 15, 17, 19, 21,
     33, 38, 39, 49, 56, 60, 62, 65,
     68, 69, 72, 76, 77, 79, 80, 82,
     85
   Books on 124, 127–8
   Stories from 132–3
Church of England 13, 15, 39, 41
Circle time 82
Circular 3/89 36
Collective worship 20–1, 34, 40,
     48, 66
Continity 84
Cowper-Temple Clause 33

Dearing Report 64
Determination, a 40

Education Act, 1944 1, 34, 35, 41, 47, 88
Education Reform Act, 1988 1, 12, 35, 37–42, 53, 66, 81, 82, 85, 88
entitlement curriculum 1, 69, 70, 95

Faith Working Parties 43
Foundation Subjects 23, 36

Goldman, Ronald 34–5
Grant maintained schools 43
Great Britain 37, 41
Gurudwaras 35, 49, 72

Headteachers 12, 13, 14, 15, 64, 65, 68
Her Majesty's Inspectors 1
Hinduism (Hindus) 17, 22, 35, 41, 49, 63, 65, 77, 80, 82
Books on 124, 128–9
Stories from 133–4
Humanists 40, 41, 51
Humanities 14

ICT 142–3
INSET 25, 26, 70
Islam (Muslim) 15, 22, 35, 41, 49, 51, 52, 60, 65, 72, 77, 82
Books on 124–5, 129
Stories from 134–5

Judaism (Jewish) 35, 41, 52, 77, 78, 79, 82
Books on 125, 130
Stories from 134

Local Education Authorities 37, 38, 40–2, 81

Mandir 49, 72
Methodist Church 41
Model Syllabuses 39, 43, 81, 85
Monitoring RE 23, 24, 28, 106–11

Mosque 35, 49, 72, 114
Multicultural issues 11, 14, 21

National Curriculum 8, 9, 22, 23, 36, 37, 62, 66, 81, 96–7, 117
National Secular Society 48
New Churches, The 41

Orthodox Churches, The 41

Planning RE
long term 85, 95, 96–7, 98–104
medium term 95, 96, 97, 105
short term 95, 96, 105
PSHE 82
Photopacks 141, 154–6
Posters 141, 154–6
Principal religious traditions 7, 37–8, 41, 42, 56
Progression 86
Publishers of RE material 153–4

QCA 40

Recording 115–16
Religion 9, 15, 60, 68, 70, 73, 75, 76
as a seven dimensional activity 73–81, 86
Religious Education Coordinators
lack of knowledge 23–4
problems encountered 12, 20–3
qualifications 11, 13
reasons for appointment 14–15
Research Project 11–29
role 2, 3, 7–10
satisfactions of the job 12, 16–20
anticipated future needs 12, 25–9
Religious Education Policy 22, 23, 24, 26, 28, 67, 68, 72, 88–91

Religious Education Resource
Centres 152–3
Religious Education Scheme of
Work 18, 22, 23, 24, 67, 97
Religious Instruction 34, 39, 47,
48
Religious Society of Friends, The
41
Reporting 116
Resources 18, 23, 24, 26–8, 66,
85, 110, 153
*see also* artefacts, books,
photopacks, posters
Roman Catholic Church 41

SACRE 40–2
Salvation Army 41
SCAA 39
Sikhism (Sikh) 43, 49, 63, 77
Books about 125, 130–1
Stories from 135

Smart, Ninian 71, 81
Spiritual and moral
awareness/development 46,
52, 53–5
Standing Conference 41, 42, 43
Subject leader 2

Teacher attitudes to RE 9–10,
20–2, 59–63

United Reformed Church 41

Videos 142
Visits to places of worship 17,
67, 85, 86, 144–6
Visitors 27, 86, 146–50
Voluntary aided schools 11, 42
Voluntary controlled schools 42

Withdrawal from RE 8, 34, 37,
48

# ORDER FORM

**Post**: *Customer Services Department, Falmer Press, Rankine Road, Basingstoke, Hampshire, RG24 8PR*
**Tel**: *(01256) 813000* **Fax**: *(01256) 479438*
**E-mail**: *book.orders@tandf.co.uk*

**10% DISCOUNT AND FREE P&P FOR SCHOOLS OR INDIVIDUALS ORDERING THE COMPLETE SET ORDER YOUR SET NOW. WITH CREDIT CARD PAYMENTS, YOU WON'T BE CHARGED TILL DESPATCH.**

| TITLE | DUE | ISBN | PRICE | QTY |
|---|---|---|---|---|
| **SUBJECT LEADERS' HANDBOOKS SET** | | **(RRP £207.20)** | **£185.00** | |
| Coordinating Science | 2/98 | 0 7507 0688 0 | £12.95 | |
| Coordinating Design and Technology | 2/98 | 0 7507 0689 9 | £12.95 | |
| Coordinating Maths | 2/98 | 0 7507 0687 2 | £12.95 | |
| Coordinating Physical Education | 2/98 | 0 7507 0693 7 | £12.95 | |
| Coordinating History | 2/98 | 0 7507 0691 0 | £12.95 | |
| Coordinating Music | 2/98 | 0 7507 0694 5 | £12.95 | |
| Coordinating Geography | 2/98 | 0 7507 0692 9 | £12.95 | |
| Coordinating English at Key Stage 1 | 4/98 | 0 7507 0685 6 | £12.95 | |
| Coordinating English at Key Stage 2 | 4/98 | 0 7507 0686 4 | £12.95 | |
| Coordinating IT | 4/98 | 0 7507 0690 2 | £12.95 | |
| Coordinating Art | 4/98 | 0 7507 0695 3 | £12.95 | |
| Coordinating Religious Education | Late 98 | 0 7507 0613 9 | £12.95 | |
| Management Skills for SEN Coordinators | Late 98 | 0 7507 0697 X | £12.95 | |
| Building a Whole School Assessment Policy | Late 98 | 0 7507 0698 8 | £12.95 | |
| Curriculum Coordinator and OFSTED Inspection | Late 98 | 0 7507 0699 6 | £12.95 | |
| Coordinating Curriculum in Smaller Primary School | Late 98 | 0 7507 0700 3 | £12.95 | |

I wish to pay by:

❏ Cheque *(Pay Falmer Press)*

❏ Pro-forma invoice

❏ Credit Card *(Mastercard / Visa / AmEx)*

**\*Please add p&p**
*orders up to £25*    *10%*
*orders from £25 to £50*    *5%*
*orders over £50*    *free*

| | |
|---|---|
| **Value of Books** | |
| **P&P\*** | |
| **Total** | |

*Card Number* _____ *Expiry Date* _____

*Signature* _____

*Name* _____ *Title/Position* _____

*School* _____

*Address* _____

*Postcode* _____ *Country* _____

*Tel no.* _____ *Fax* _____

*E-mail* _____

❏ If you do not wish to receive further promotional information from the Taylor&Francis Group, please tick box.
All prices are correct at time of going to print but may change without notice

**Ref: 1197BFSLAD**